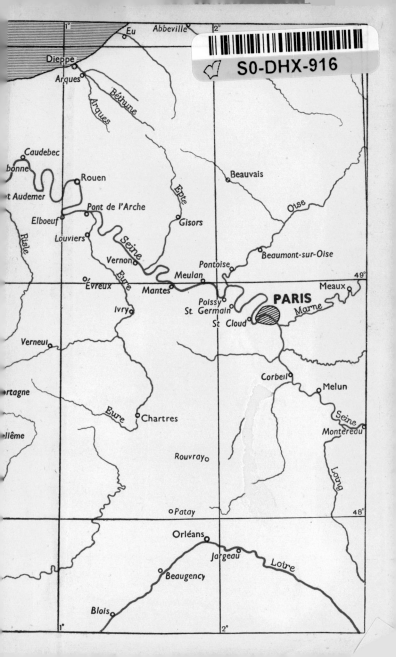

HENRY V

and the

Invasion of France

is one of the volumes
in the
TEACH YOURSELF HISTORY
LIBRARY

Edited by A. L. ROWSE

Teach Yourself History

HENRY V.

HENRY V

and the

Invasion of France

by

E. F. JACOB

Published by

HODDER & STOUGHTON LIMITED

for THE ENGLISH UNIVERSITIES PRESS

AT SAINT PAUL'S HOUSE

IN THE CITY OF LONDON

FIRST PRINTED 1947

To G. E. LARMAN

A General Introduction to the Series

THIS series has been undertaken in the conviction that there can be no subject of study more important than history. Great as have been the conquests of natural science in our time —such that many think of ours as a scientific age *par excellence*—it is even more urgent and necessary that advances should be made in the social sciences, if we are to gain control of the forces of nature loosed upon us. The bed out of which all the social sciences spring is history; there they find, in greater or lesser degree, subject-matter and material, verification or contradiction.

There is no end to what we can learn from history, if only we would, for it is coterminous with life. Its special field is the life of man in society, and at every point we can learn vicariously from the experience of others before us in history.

To take one point only—the understanding of politics: how can we hope to understand the world of affairs around us if we do not know how it came to be what it is? How to understand Germany, or Soviet Russia, or the United States —or ourselves, without knowing something of their history?

There is no subject that is more useful, or indeed indispensable.

Some evidence of the growing awareness of this may be seen in the immense increase in the interest of the reading public in history, and the much larger place the subject has come to take in education in our time.

This series has been planned to meet the needs and demands of a very wide public and of education—they are indeed the same. I am convinced that the most congenial, as well as the most concrete and practical, approach to history is the biographical, through the lives of the great men whose actions have been so much part of history, and whose careers in turn have been so moulded and formed by events.

The key-idea of this series, and what distinguishes it from any other that has appeared, is the intention by way of a biography of a great man to open up a significant historical theme; for example, Cromwell and the Puritan Revolution, or Lenin and the Russian Revolution.

My hope is, in the end, as the series fills out and completes itself, by a sufficient number of biographies to cover whole periods and subjects in that way. To give you the history of the United States, for example, or the British Empire or France, *via* a number of biographies of their leading historical figures.

That should be something new, as well as convenient and practical, in education.

I need hardly say that I am a strong believer in people with good academic standards writing once more for the general reading public, and of the public being given the best that the universities can provide. From this point of view this series is intended to bring the university into the homes of the people.

A. L. ROWSE.

ALL SOULS COLLEGE,
    OXFORD.

Note

FOR some years, while at Manchester, I was engaged with a group of young historians upon the chronicle and record sources of Henry V's reign. The following chapters are a condensation of that work (mainly where it touched relations with France), in as simple a form as I could contrive, with footnotes and the apparatus of learning for the most part omitted. The first two pages reveal the objectives of the little book.

I should like to thank my friend, Mr. A. R. Myers, of the University of Liverpool, for reading and commenting upon it at an earlier stage.

E. F. JACOB.

ALL SOULS COLLEGE
OXFORD.

Contents

Chapter One

Introductory

WHEN in the early hours of 6 June, 1944 glider-borne troops and parachutists of the allied armies descended upon the coast lands of Lower Normandy, they were marking out the path of re-conquest trodden by Henry V just over 500 years before. Henry's first attempt to recover the duchy—his own duchy, he always said—though it ended with the victory of Agincourt and the dispersal of a great French army, was abortive: his forces were too small, too stricken with disease and too tired to hold even a narrow maritime strip from Calais to the Seine. His second effort, carried out in more or less the same area as the armies of General Eisenhower, led to momentous results: the conquest of France almost up to the Loire, and the establishment of an Anglo-Burgundian domination in Paris, the centre of the French monarchy. In the Treaty of Troyes the English and French crowns were united, a dual monarchy was created, and to all appearances an independent France was no more. There was to be the one Anglo-French kingdom, the union of states proposed (though under what profoundly different

I

circumstances!) to France by Mr. Churchill's government in 1940. This was Henry V's bid to solve for ever the problem of Anglo-French relations: it was the *voie de fait*, the forcible solution. Before a generation was out, it had, as we know, broken down.

The story raises two historical issues of capital importance: the personality and aims of a great war leader, Harry of England; and the fundamental nature of Anglo-French relations during the course of our early history. The former is a strictly historical theme; but the latter leads, even at this distance of time, to political generalizations. The history of England's relation with France as a formal matter of embassies and marching and heraldry has its own fascination, as all readers of Froissart will appreciate; but if the subject is to be really felt and experienced, if it is to engage more than the memory, it must penetrate deeply into the character of the two peoples, reveal the one to the other, and lead to understanding of the differences that existed and may always exist. We may and we should criticize one another, as long as we do not shut up our hearts:

> Frères humains, qui après nous vivez,
> N'ayez les cuers contre nous endurcis,
> Car, se pitié de nous povres avez,
> Dieu en aura plus tost de vous mercis.

To Shakespeare most people owe their intro-

duction to the character and personality, of
Henry V. It is a sound introduction, so long as
the dramatist's point of view is understood.
Drawing largely upon Edward Hall's history,
styled *The Union of the two Noble and Illustre
Families of Lancaster and York*, Shakespeare had
always in mind the contrast between the union
and peace that flourished in Henry VIII's day
and the unhappy and unnatural divisions of
Lancaster and York. The trouble began with the
quarrel of Hereford and Norfolk in *Richard II*; it
continued (in *Henry IV*) with the revolt of the
Percies and Archbishop Scrope's rebellion; and
it worked itself out to a bitter and tragic conclusion first in the rivalry of Beaufort and
Gloucester, then in the machinations of the
stormy Margaret of Anjou, and finally in the
able but self-thwarting Richard III. But one
oasis of agreement, one anticipation of united
national sentiment lay in the middle of the long
story, unfolded (though not in order of composition) in the historical plays. The self-willed
Henry of Monmouth who would have snatched
the crown from his stricken father, became, once
the 'offending Adam' was whipped out of him,
the embodiment of the purest patriotism; unself-
seeking, free from vanity, the paragon of honour
and bravery. In Henry V, Shakespeare has
portrayed the true monarch of Elizabethan
idealism, a figure dominant over State and
Church alike, an instrument of the divine will.

3

After Agincourt he can exclaim:

> O God, thy arm was here,
> And not to us, but to thy arm alone
> Ascribe we all.

Yet, as the unforgettable night scene with Williams and Bates before the battle shows, it was a divine instrument with very human perceptions, quick to understand the morale of his troops, disquieted with responsibilities that did not disturb the sleep of humbler folk:

> For though I speak it, I think the King is but a man, as I am: the violet smells to him as it doth to me; the element shows to him as it doth to me; all his senses have but human conditions: his ceremonies laid by, in his nakedness he appears but a man; and though his affections are higher mounted than ours, yet, when they stoop, they stoop with the like wing. (Act IV. Sc. i.)

This is the king who by his humanity as well as his high purpose had quickened the national pulse and raised the country to unity and self-respect by his honourable struggle against France:

> Now all the youth of England are on fire,
> And silken dalliance in the wardrobe lies:
> Now thrive the armorers and honour's thought
> Reigns solely in the breast of every man:
> They sell the pasture now to buy the horse;

Following the mirror of all Christian kings,
With winged heels, as English Mercuries.

(Act i. Sc. ii.)

The excitement is infectious: yet there are
doubts about the glowing picture. The reaction
against the prince whom Shakespeare makes
repudiate Sir John Falstaff, his old drinking
companion, has gone deep. One important
political aim the dramatist attributes to his
expeditions, namely to unify the country by a
forward, aggressive policy against France and
Scotland, and so to divert 'giddy minds' from
supporting the Lollard offensive against Church
endowments, seems hardly in keeping with the
purity of Henry's motives. The modern tendency
has been to regard his negotiations with the
French diplomatists from 1414 to 1416 as little
more than (in Dr. Wylie's words) 'a hollow
sham', covering intensive preparation for war.
His sudden conversion to gravity and sobriety
at his accession has been termed priggishness
and hypocrisy; the magnificent diction of the
speeches put into his mouth is thought to conceal
sheer predatory nationalism; his territorial and
dynastic claims upon France to lack all justification. In the notable film version of *Henry V* the
speech of the Archbishop of Canterbury on the
Salic Law and the Plantagenet claim to the
French throne has been burlesqued in a manner
to suggest that it was a tedious and pedantic

5

formality, since Henry, when he asked for a legal statement, had already determined upon war. While it is more than doubtful that the speech was ever in fact delivered, no Tudor audience would have thought the Archbishop's careful citation of authorities a fit subject for merriment; and the fact that Shakespeare makes a king of a recently usurping dynasty ask for a statement of his legal rights against France as if he were a direct linear descendant of the original claimant, shows a true reading of the Lancastrian mind. Naturally, Shakespeare has to portray the French case as weak, the English as overwhelming: the play must move swiftly to France, and long balancing delays and debates be excluded, so that, to the moralist, Henry V's agreement with the belligerent temper of his *entourage* is cynically quick; nevertheless a critical estimate, while it may have many reservations, is likely to support the Henry of Shakespeare (just as in general outline it has endorsed his Richard II) as a true figure of history, acting justifiably according to the needs and the standards of his time.

In the minds of the English upper classes during the Middle Ages France aroused conflicting emotions. She was both a clever, sophisticated adversary, and a school of chivalry and deportment. The whole history of Anglo-French relations illustrates the theme of alternative enmity and attraction: the latter frequently predominant. England was a small and a 'much governed' country; apart from occasional tournaments and petty skirmishes on the Welsh and Scottish marches, opportunities for military training and adventure were scanty. France, on the other hand, was a wider field, offering the young noble the chance of service under relatives or family friends, and later, when England and France were at conflict, plentiful scope for training upon the expeditions and *chevauchées*, or raids, that made up a great deal of the Hundred Years War. Under Henry II, for instance, young William Marshal was first sent as a squire to his father's cousin, the Chamberlain of Tancarville, a powerful baron with castle on the lower Seine, and took part in a campaign against the French king's forces in the county of Eu. He then followed his uncle to Poitou to suppress a revolt of the nobles led by the Counts of La Marche and Angoulême, and later on was military tutor to Henry Fitz Henry, participating in his master's rebellion against the English King. An able young English knight was keenly sought after by the vassals of the French king, and might take service with one, whether he fought for the Capetian monarch or against him in the interests of the House of Anjou. Along with his military education, the young adventurer would learn to admire the standards of knightly culture specially associated with French courts; he would appreciate the romances which gave them expression, and perhaps himself practise, if a little diffidently, the art of courtly love. English nobles commonly spoke French; French (in the Anglo-Norman form) was the language of the law courts; a French higher clergy had come to England as the result of the Norman conquest; and English architecture, with the arrival of William of Sens to rebuild Canterbury Cathedral, took and developed—though in its own particular idiom—modes from across the sea. It was an age when the state, in the modern sense of the word, was scarcely known: when a 'foreigner' meant not necessarily somebody from abroad, but someone from a district not one's own. A feudal baronage with branches on both sides of the Channel was the dominant force in society; and the western church, rising under Alexander III and his immediate successors to the height of its prestige, maintained the international spirit.

This was the position during the first century and a half after the Norman Conquest, at any rate till the loss of the Duchy of Normandy in 1204. During this time England became, through the marriage of Henry of Anjou with Eleanor of Aquitaine, part of a great continental empire whose centre was the Loire valley rather than Westminster: a huge area covering territories from the borders of Ponthieu in the north to the Pyrenean fiefs of Béarn, Bigorre and Comminges in the south. Henry II was a continental monarch (why else should he lie buried at Fontévrault?)

as much at home in Tours or Angers as in West-minster. The methods used by his chanceries were Angevin, their personnel drawn from all parts of his empire. Although the French kings claimed homage for the duchies and fiefs that originally formed part of the Western Carolingian kingdom, for all practical purposes the Angevin state was independent. If the loss of Normandy to Philip Augustus forced the Anglo-Norman baronage to choose which side they preferred to serve, national sentiment was as yet so rudi-mentary that in 1216 the English barons called in Prince Louis, son of Philip Augustus, to help them against their own King John, and even from 1258-1264 English reforming elements of every rank were prepared to accept the leader-ship of a Frenchman, Simon de Montfort. It is common to contrast the institutions of the two countries : but such emphasis on the discrepancies often fails to bring out how much that is commonly thought characteristic of England—the sworn inquest, for example, the early municipal council, the mayoralty, the office of escheator—was due to continental influence, whether Norman or Angevin. And there was the great magnet of the schools of Chartres, Orléans, and Paris, which drew some of the best minds from England, and either retained them as teachers or sent them back to impart the theological wisdom of the greatest university in the west to simpler English clerks.

So strong were the affinities that the development of a national consciousness on either side was a slow process. In England it came after the loss of Normandy, with the greater integration of the country, when the middle and lower middle ranks of society began to take a more active part in the judicial and administrative life of the community. This process, normally associated with the thirteenth and fourteenth centuries, was not complete until the presence and consultation of the commons in parliament became a normal part of our constitutional machinery. It was in such an assembly that the king's need for financial assistance against his enemies could be expressed in forcible terms through the 'pronouncement of parliament' or opening address setting forth the causes of summons; and as the taxes on movables demanded there touched small as well as great, ventilation and discussion of the circumstances and the urgency of the grant were inevitable. Policy and initiative in foreign affairs were, of course, entirely the king's; the discussion of foreign relations was a major interest of the King's Council, which might or might not seek the advice or approval of the magnates in parliament; but if the commons had to shoulder part of the expenses of any decision, it was good policy at least to outline to them the object of their contribution, and to do so with art and appeal. There is a basic similarity between Edward I and Philip IV in the propagandist use of their assemblies; but while in England parliament became a more regularly meeting and a more articulate body than its French neighbour, owing to the king's insistence on receiving precise and definite promises in reply to his demands, in France it was not the Estates that mobilized opinion so much as the royal administrators themselves in their enthusiasm for their master's rights. The unity of France came through the expansion of the domainal administration, as it insinuated itself through its agents wherever the king's rights could be claimed: not in compact territorial blocks, but piecemeal, till outpost could be linked to outpost, and each joined to the central administration at Paris. It was a process of steady infiltration, involving constant frontier incidents and legal claims. Faced with the challenge of the English possessions in France, the Capetians from the time of Philip Augustus onwards detached fief by fief from the English allegiance by an opportunist policy which won admiration for its technique, while in time it came to be shielded by the reputation for justice and sanctity which was the legacy of St. Louis to the French crown.

The first serious attempt at a general solution of Anglo-French differences was the Treaty of Paris (1259). This was a most carefully drawn document, the foundation of all diplomatic intercourse during the next eighty years. By it

St. Louis granted Henry III a number of fiefs and territories in, or on, the borders of Aquitaine, and in return Henry promised to hold these lands, as well as his existing Duchy of Gascony, in liege homage as Duke of Aquitaine and peer of France. He also renounced all right to Normandy, Anjou, Touraine and Poitou. This settlement meant the liquidation of the old Angevin Empire, and the creation of a new southern French feudal kingdom held by the English monarch from the king of France; but the transfer of the fiefs to Henry III raised acute problems, since most of the lands were not actually in the French king's possession. For example, St. Louis gave Henry all the land that he held in fiefs or demesne in the bishoprics of Limoges, Cahors and Périgueux, save for the homage of his brothers, should they possess any holding in these territories. Similarly Henry was to have lands in Quercy held by Alphonse of Poitiers, brother of St. Louis, in right of his wife Joan of Poitiers, provided that it could be established by inquiry that Richard Coeur de Lion had granted them to Joan of England when she married Raymond VI, Count of Toulouse and grandfather of Joan of Poitiers. The execution of the treaty depended therefore upon the solution of a number of confused and difficult questions, involving minute enquiries and the presentation of a mass of historical evidence. The homage also caused the greatest difficulties.

The English thesis, utterly denied by France, was that the act was conditional upon the terms of the Treaty of Paris being carried out, and later, when a further settlement had been reached, upon the French remedying certain infractions. These and other acts of pillage and piracy on either side were the subject of claim and counter-claim in the periods between the successive acts of homage, and no satisfactory solution of the grievances or clear termination of the territorial muddle was ever arrived at.

The years of diplomatic negotiation between 1259 and 1339 saw two important developments. One was the creation of an office of diplomatic administration with a staff of clerks directed by the *Custos processuum* or Keeper of Processes (the 'process' being a meeting for the settlement of outstanding diplomatic questions, much as we speak of Yalta or Potsdam), who was a sort of under-secretary for foreign affairs. From his records, exhaustively kept, every case and claim could be presented with a mass of detail. It was his business to prepare the *dossier* for the embassies or missions that negotiated with any foreign power. In the negotiations with France, both sides early became expert (alas! perhaps too expert) in the minutiæ of the past. They were too well served by their clerical staffs who supplied the data from the archives for the long pro-tracted disputes. The other development was the growing recognition, as the fourteenth century

advanced, that no result could ever come from
peaceful diplomatic negotiations with the French,
whom it seemed impossible to pin down. On
each occasion the English negotiations claimed
to have met with evasion or positive counter-
claim. The knot could only be cut by forcible
methods, and it was Edward III's aim, as soon
as his personal government began, to keep
France quiet until his preparations had been
made and a great coalition built up along her
eastern frontiers.

Looking back, we can see where the real
trouble lay: it was the steady pressure of the
French royal officials in Gascony and the
encouragement they gave to the southern French
feudatories of the English king to act in the
interest of their overlord at Paris. Under Henry
III the English seneschal of Gascony [1] was kept
short of supplies and had little help from the
home government. Edward I tried to rectify
the position by a great inquiry defining his
feudal rights, as well as by the creation of
defensive posts or *bastides* at various points: but
these positions only led to further sniping and
border warfare which increased in Edward II's
reign. Under Philip IV and Charles IV the
position of an English king who was duke of
Gascony became increasingly difficult. 'As
Gascon duke he was obliged to resist the French

---

[1] The seneschal or steward of Gascony was the King's
lieutenant in that Duchy.

king's application to that region of the same policy of monarchical centralization that he himself, as English king, was applying with all his strength in his own insular dominions'. This was the fundamental cause of the Hundred Years War, when England sought to break out of the diplomatic entanglement. Previously she had been forced back upon it whenever the question of a general settlement arose, for not only was she too well served by her archivists, but she had confronting her an opponent even more skilled in procedural delay and the use of technicalities and diplomatic precedent.

Influencing the course of the war were three factors without which Lancastrian policy towards France cannot be understood. The first was the direct result of Edward III's attempt to secure the Flemish towns as his allies against the French king: the claim to the French throne. Flanders was a fief of France, with a pro-French court and a pro-French aristocracy: but its industrial bourgeoisie, engaged in cloth-making, was dependent for its livelihood on the free importation of English wool. To prohibit such imports and invite Flemish weavers to settle in England was not sufficient to induce the towns to throw in their lot with Edward: they had to be assured that they had good legal grounds for opposing their overlord. They had to see Edward III replace Philip of Valois as the true successor to King Charles of France in virtue of his mother being heiress to her deceased brother and capable of transmitting the succession. The claim which his predecessor Edward II had seriously considered making, was not simply 'a hollow party move'. If diplomatic circumstances had evoked it, none the less it was to form a vital part of the English case against France and to colour all subsequent negotiations. It formed the basis of a great official collection of documents on English foreign relations, put together in the fifteenth century as the *Liber Recordorum* or 'Book of the royal evidences and records', extracts from which have been copied into a number of surviving manuscripts. The claim may have arisen to satisfy formal legality: it ended by being believed in and stoutly upheld.

The second was the humiliating Treaty of Calais [1] (1360) which closed the first phase of the war after the defeat and capture of King John at Poitiers. For John's ransom the terms prescribed the huge figure of 3,000,000 gold crowns, the payment of which was to be spread over six years. The territorial clauses were equally severe. The whole duchy of Aquitaine, including Poitou in the north, Rouergue in the east, Bigorre and Béarn in the south, was added to England (already holding Gascony), together with Calais and the surrounding country of

---

[1] Commonly called, from its preliminaries (May 1360) the Treaty of Brétigny. We refer to it as such. See map at end of volume.

Guines as well as Ponthieu, Queen Philippa's inheritance. These were terms agreed at Brétigny in May 1360, and it was there settled that the English claim to the French throne should be withdrawn, in return for which the French king should renounce all rights of suzerainty over the districts ceded to Edward III. When the treaty was finally issued at Calais in October 1360 the operation of this dynastic clause was postponed pending the restoration of territories. The clause never took effect: the claim continued and French suzerainty over Aquitaine was never specifically renounced. The situation after the Treaty of Paris might almost be said to have repeated itself. Meanwhile the monstrous indemnity hung like a millstone round the neck of France. The treaty is important because, in subsequent negotiations, as we shall see, the English government constantly reverted to its territorial and financial clauses, and because in Calais it established a bastion of immense economic and strategic importance just across the channel, giving an opportunity to control the narrow seas.

The third factor was the disastrous civil strife which began after the death of Charles V of France. When war broke out again after a nine years peace (1369) Charles and his captain Du Guesclin brought about a revival of French military power, while the naval defeat at La Rochelle (1372) was a disastrous blow to this country. But it was a severe and oppressive régime for France, especially in taxation, only tolerable under a careful and far-seeing monarch. His successor, Charles VI, a pathetic figure, later subject to fits of insanity, was no such person. Under him first the King's uncles, then his brother Louis, duke of Touraine, controlled policy and the government. Louis, who was married to Valentina Visconti, daughter of the powerful Gian Galeazzo, Visconti of Milan, turned French eyes to Italy and the Mediterranean. He planned to accept Clement VII's offer to enfeoff him with a kingdom carved out of the Papal States, on condition of driving out the rival pope in the Great Schism. At the same time Charles VI was induced to support the claim of his cousin, Louis of Anjou, to Naples and Sicily. There was to be a vast expedition to Italy, led by Charles VI, to establish these claimants in their new territories (1390). Had it materialized, it might have led to French domination in Italy and the indefinite prolongation of the Schism. It was these Italian schemes, along with the oppressive and prodigal régime of Louis of Touraine, now Duke of Orléans, that aroused the opposition of Philip the Good, Duke of Burgundy, Charles V's brother, and led to the permanent antagonism, on almost every ground of policy, between his successor, John the Fearless and Count Bernard of Armagnac, leader of the Orléanist party after the murder

(1407), by Burgundian agents, of the Duke of Orléans. This event extinguished all hope of reconciliation between Burgundy and the three royal dukes, Berry, Bourbon and Brittany, who had embraced the cause of the deceased Orléans. Both sides looked round for allies, and in 1411 appealed to Henry IV's government.

During the early part of Richard II's reign English policy, largely swayed by John of Gaunt, had been to strike at France through her allies, rather than directly. (The French had learned the lessons Du Guesclin had taught them, and systematically avoided pitched battles or large engagements. They had come to respect the power of the English archers on these occasions.) The campaigns undertaken by England against the Clementine party in Flanders, in Scotland and in Castile were intended as indirect blows, while France could be lulled into unsuspecting security by truces and negotiations, until the time was ripe for a greater and more decisive attack. But Richard II, when he came to terms with his Council and undertook the government personally, made the first serious attempt at an understanding that might have led to a definite peace. After the death of his queen, Anne of Bohemia, he asked for the hand of Charles V's daughter, Isabel, and in 1396 the two were betrothed. Secretly he wanted French help in case of need, to pursue his grudge against the Appellants, but he was also genuinely desirous of alliance with a court which appealed to his tastes and aesthetic sensibility. The truce already made was prolonged for twenty-eight years, and it was the profoundest misfortune for the two countries that these should have been the years of sharpest division within France. A strong and united French administration could then have made, upon reasonable terms, a peace with England which might have lasted throughout the fifteenth century. But to negotiate with the court of Charles VI was to negotiate with whichever party was in the ascendant, and there was no hope of continuity. This division within the direction of French policy is largely responsible for the charges made by English chroniclers and writers against the French for duplicity. *Gallicana duplicitas* becomes the regular accusation: the French were 'double-dealers', but the real reason was the existence of two sets of counsels within, rather than conscious deception. It was through that division that the English came once more into France.

From either faction the offer to England had to be a substantial one. Burgundy's main promises were in the north. England was always nervous about the position of Calais, the first place to be threatened in any war with France; she was equally anxious to keep open the trade with Flanders, so frequently endangered by the acts of piracy committed by her merchants. When in July 1411 John the Fearless asked for

English aid in resisting the Dukes of Orléans and Berry, he professed himself ready to hand over four of his Flemish towns, Gravelines, Dunkirk, Dixmuiden and Sluys, and to help the English to reconquer Normandy. He also proposed to give his daughter Anne in marriage to the Prince of Wales. Nothing was said about the English claims, under the Treaty of Brétigny, to Aquitaine; nor was it stated whether the duke would be prepared to take arms against his own sovereign and so turn a private war against his opponents into something very much bigger. The Armagnac offer, in January 1412, was on a larger scale, and promised much of the South. The French lords who made it undertook to recognize the King of England as their superior lord for all Aquitaine, to admit English troops into the chief towns, and to hand over the territories upon the death of their respective holders. This applied also to Poitou, at the time in the hands of the Duke of Berry, and to Angoulême which was held by the Duke of Orléans. The English king was therefore to have the reversion of much that he was claiming, while the rest was to be handed over to him, with their active assistance, when he brought or sent his army to France to assist them against Burgundy. This was an appeal to English southward ambitions along the old lines.

Henry IV tried both plans. The Burgundian alliance, though the marriage negotiations never got anywhere, was favoured by the Prince of Wales, who had secured the ascendancy in the Council over the Arundel ministry, and the English force that was sent found itself assisting Burgundy to defeat the Armagnacs in the Paris neighbourhood at the bridge of St. Cloud. It was a limited campaign of two months, and the duke intended it to be the preliminary to greater operations. But before it could be followed up, the prince had been displaced by Archbishop Arundel with the support of Thomas, the king's second son, and dismissed from the Council. The promise of Aquitaine was too tempting to be resisted, and on 15 May, 1412 a treaty, bitterly opposed by the prince, was concluded with the Armagnac lords, in virtue of which a considerable English force was dispatched to the continent. But the army never got much farther than the Loire. In July the Dukes of Berry, Orléans and Bourbon came to terms with Burgundy (now posing patriotically as the supporter of the French king against the invader), and in November the English were bought out and withdrew to Aquitaine. It was an inglorious ending to a carefully prepared expedition, and the prince, after his succession to the throne, was to make good use of the documents by which the Armagnac lords promised England, in return for its assistance, the territories that once formed part of the Angevin Empire of Henry II. It is likely that his experiences in 1411 and 1412 determined

him to try, once again as in 1259 and 1360, the
path of a general settlement: but a settlement
lacking the unsatisfactory territorial clauses, the
ambiguities of homage and overlordship in the
earlier documents: one, in fact, imposed by force
if it could not be negotiated by agreement.

Chapter Two

The Prince

THE young king, who in March 1413 succeeded
his father, was twenty-five (b. 16 September,
1387). When Henry of Bolingbroke, then Duke
of Hereford, was banished and suffered the
confiscation of his estates (1398), Richard II
assumed charge of his young cousin, and along
with Humphrey of Gloucester took him over to
Ireland (May 1399), where he was knighted.
Richard liked the boy, and the feeling was
evidently mutual, for one of the first acts of
Henry, when king, was to bring Richard's body
from King's Langley to be honourably interred at
Westminster. Very soon after his father's accession his official career began. On 15 October, 1399
he was created Prince of Wales, Duke of Cornwall
and Earl of Chester; on 23 October, Duke of
Aquitaine, and on 10 November he was given
the Duchy of Lancaster, a step that was to unite
the Duchy with the crown, though its administrative organization was, and remained, wholly
separate. He was only just thirteen when he was
put in charge of the government of North Wales
and the Marches: this was, in point of fact,
exercised by a Council of which Henry Percy

(Hotspur), Justiciar of North Wales, was the leading member. His own personal governor was at first Sir Hugh le Despencer, succeeded at the end of 1401 by Thomas Percy, Earl of Worcester.

The late Mr. C. L. Kingsford observed that 'with the actual government of Wales the prince himself had little to do'. The boy would naturally follow the advice of the governors and leading members of the Council: yet it is worth noting that by the time he was eighteen Henry had made himself the leading military captain in the west; and we are fortunate to possess, in an All Souls College manuscript, a good deal of his Welsh correspondence[1], showing that he was by no means a mere figure-head. From it the sort of training and experience he was getting can be seen. Henry IV's government, when they sent him there, can scarcely have realized the growing power of Owen Glendower's movement: it took time to appreciate the national character of the uprising. In the early years while Owen was fighting his way southwards and attaching first Edmund Mortimer and later Henry Percy to his cause, we can see from Prince Henry's letters both the military incidents and the day-to-day governmental work done in his name. In June 1401, for instance, John Charlton, Lord of Powys, tells Henry that while he was marching north-east to Denbigh his men had nearly caught Owen in the

---

[1] No. 182. The letters are printed by M. D. Legge, *Anglo-Norman Letters and Petitions*, p. 280 f.

mountains, but that when attacked, the enemy
ran, leaving some armour behind and a cloth
'painted with maidens with red hands'—a fine
barbaric touch. Rebellion might flare up anywhere,
particularly in the disaffected parts of South
Wales, to which Owen transferred himself after
his encounter with Powys. A follower of Owen
has murdered an English official and must be
punished for it, 'or otherwise it does not behove
any Englishman henceforth to be an official in
Wales'. Then, on a more peaceful topic, two
tenants have complained that they cannot possess
themselves of a cargo of wine in the *George*, the
ship of a Chester mariner, which is detained by
the authorities for breaking arrest, and the prince
orders the wine to be delivered.

At the same time Henry IV is constantly
informing the prince of events that may concern
him: a great assembly of Owen and his people;
the imperative need to relieve Harlech Castle,
which is being besieged by the rebels, since it is
cheaper to keep a castle than re-take it. The
king kept in very close touch with his son,
informed him of all Welsh appointments, exhorted
him to work in closest co-operation with his
council. In return the boy consulted his father on
every matter of importance. The prince regularly
received reports from his senior officers. One will
tell Henry that he is holding the sessions in South
Wales, and that Cardigan and Caermarthen are
submitting, but that he needs an English justice

to help him in the work, and suggests a name. The prince's own letters have a strong individuality, and show a virile grasp of a difficult situation; and some of the more personal ones reveal his character. Writing to a bishop, he asks pardon for one of his servants who has been excommunicated for having allowed some of his dogs to kill five wild animals in the bishop's Sussex park, and expresses his displeasure against such a trespass 'against you or any other person of the holy church'; adding that if the offence is repeated, the bishop is to sue the common law against the delinquent, 'for he will not be sustained or maintained by us in any way touching such matters'—in pleasant and striking contrast to the insolent young Henry of legend who tries to protect one of his servants from the Chief Justice. On the other hand, he is prepared to save certain villeins from amercement by the justice of North Wales, because the services they had been required to perform were not customary. He suppresses profiteering by arresting certain Chester citizens for refusing to sell oats to the prince's purveyors save at fancy prices (*sans ce qu'ils leur paient es mains à leur plaiser*). These details, sometimes trivial in themselves, show that Henry of Monmouth was very far from being the prince of the Boar's Head Tavern.

All the time finance was the bugbear. If the king and his treasurer John Norbury were continually short of money, the prince's need was equally great. When in 1403 he was appointed his father's lieutenant in the Marches of Wales, he had to represent his poverty to the council in the strongest terms, and he constantly recurred to the theme. Payment was one of the weakest points of a medieval army or garrison: Henry IV's commitments were so many that it was a constant struggle to get priority for Wales. The Commons who made the grants scarcely realised the need for a permanent, highly subsidised command till 1406. It was judged sufficient to conduct short campaigns in force and then melt away, leaving inadequate outposts in the Marches to deal with the vengeance of the infuriated, but by no means defeated enemy. Yet at Chester, Shrewsbury or Worcester those outposts, which had civil as well as military duties, were too far away from the mobile Welsh bands that returned when the main English army had departed. Everything turned on the energy and resources of the spasmodically paid English forces left behind: their paucity, as well as the badness of communications, helps to explain why Owen Glendower had it his own way for so long.

By 1408 the prince had been in practically every engagement of importance. He had commanded a troop of seventeen men-at-arms and ninety-nine archers in his father's invasion of Scotland (1400): in April 1403 he was in the field against Owen in the Dee valley and on the River Tanat, and got back to Shrewsbury in time to hold the ground against the Percies until the royal forces arrived, being wounded in the face by an arrow. Throughout most of 1404 he was holding on in the Marches with an absurdly small force, hampered by lack of supplies and only just able to hold the rebels in check. The corner was with difficulty turned in 1405 when in May he routed the Welsh near Usk and took prisoner Owen's son, Griffith. 1406 was the year of the tripartite convention between the Earl of Northumberland, Mortimer and Glendower, the aftermath of the rebellion in the north the previous year. Henry was not present at the slaughter of the Welsh on St. George's day (23 April), but early in June his trusted lieutenant Charlton, Lord of Powys, with the aid of the local musters of Cheshire and Shropshire, defeated Northumberland and Bardolf, and the coalition was broken up. Meanwhile he had been given command over the whole front, North and South Wales and the Marches, with power to receive and pardon all rebels, and in the autumn his commissioners were busy receiving submissions from all parts of Wales. In 1407 he was in command at the recovery of Aberystwith. Next year (September) he was back at Westminster.

He had thus weathered the critical years when the Welsh cause was linked to dynastic rebellion. Wales had taught him the value of speed and determination, the importance of supplies, and something of the siegecraft that was later to stand him in good stead. He may even have read in the third book of Egidius Colonna's *On the Government of Princes* the passages on conducting a siege, which his chaplain-biographer tells us that he had taken to heart. From Cheshire he had learned (and what companion of Richard II could fail to learn?) the value of archers, troops that he most of all cherished in his French campaigns. Above all, he had stood shoulder to shoulder with the best military leaders like the Earl of Warwick and Edward, Duke of York, and with fighting families like the Talbots and the Stanleys. He had come to prize the virtues of the marcher gentry, some of whom were to be against him in the Lollard rebellion of 1414: but they were invaluable captains in Wales, and active service blurs theological differences.

It was therefore an experienced young man who figured for the first time in the minutes of the king's council for 1408. Developments of the past thirty years had made the council a salaried and responsible body of high magnates and professional administrators. During Henry IV's increasingly frequent absences through illness, it was practically the governing authority of the kingdom. From 1407-1410 the Archbishop of Canterbury, Thomas Arundel, was the Chancellor and leading figure; but as the king's health declined, the influence of the prince and his supporters, Thomas Beaufort, Admiral of England, and Bishop Henry Beaufort of Winchester, increased. In 1410 Thomas Beaufort displaced the Chancellor, and the earls of Arundel, Westmorland and Lord Burnell came in as the lay nobles, the bishops being Beaufort of Winchester, Langley of Durham and Bubwith of Bath and Wells (all three having formerly served). Later, when Westmorland and Langley were needed in the north against the Scots, the Earl of Warwick and Bishop Henry Chichele of St. Davids were brought in. The change has sometimes been represented as a triumph for the Beaufort party which had earlier, at the hands of Arundel, suffered a reverse when the act legitimizing them had expressly excluded them from succession to the throne. Dr. Wylie was, however, right in questioning this, and in pointing out that Arundel never lost the king's favour; it was rather the prince, who was favoured by the Commons, that brought about the change, and his dominance in the Council began a positive and forward policy in external affairs.

On 18 March, 1410 he had been appointed for twelve years captain of the town of Calais (Thomas Beaufort held the castle); the change of officials there which followed this and the measures taken to strengthen the town show a new energy in the command. The Council agreed that of the forthcoming subsidy to be voted, three-quarters of the amount was to be set aside for repairing and strengthening the castle of Calais and district, and for ensuring payment for the garrison for more than two years. It was in keeping that a great deal of the expenditure warranted was military. The garrison of Berwick was at last properly supplied; the troops on the Welsh Border reinforced and properly paid, and the wages of Thomas Beaufort's sailors made up. Apart from energetic defence, the main innovation was the alliance with Burgundy and the mission of an English force to assist the duke. At all points the new régime showed the greatest energy. Henry kept the council continually at work, even on festivals, and his admirer the poet Hoccleve grumbled that there were plenty of ordinary days on which to meet, without invading holidays.

It is the more striking therefore that on 5 January, 1412 Arundel returned as Chancellor and the prince's councillors were politely discharged from their duties. The events of the next twelve months have been the subject of a legend which attributes to Henry of Monmouth the aim of securing the throne while his father was still alive. The climax of the story is the familiar scene in *Henry IV, Part II*, where in the presence of his dying father the prince tries on the crown, and his father who pardons the presumption delivers to him one of the finest of all the speeches in the historical plays. While the story of the crown-wearing is an invention of the Burgundian chronicler Monstrelet, and from him passed to Holinshed and finally to

Hall, there is a basis of fact. This is discoverable in the version of these events given by the anonymous translator of the Latin Life of Henry V by Titus Livius, the humanist and 'official' biographer of Henry. The English translator, who did his work about 1513, inserted both in his preface and in the actual text a number of stories which he had héard from his patron, the seventh earl of Ormonde. The Ormonde tales were without doubt a family inheritance from James Butler, the fourth earl (b. 1392) who went on the subsequent expedition to aid the Orleanist lords in France, and later fought with Henry V. Here and there the translator can be checked or corroborated by the St. Albans Chronicle of the monk Thomas Walsingham. The former draws attention to the slander and jealousy aroused at court not only because of the prince's conduct of his household, but also owing to 'the greate recourse of the people unto him, of whom his courte was at all times more aboundant than the Kinge his father's': the 'sinister report of some evill disposed people' suggested that 'he would usurpe the Crowne, he (Henry IV) being alive, which suspicious jealosie was occasion that he in haste withdrewe his affeccion and singular love from the prince'.

Probably at the end of 1411 Arundel was pressing for a change of policy, and Henry IV roused himself to dismiss the prince and bring back the archbishop; but the sinister suspicions may not have arisen until the new council took the step of making with the Armagnac lords an alliance which must have profoundly shocked the prince: it was then that the young Henry's opposition to such a volte-face (while English troops were still in France assisting the Duke of Burgundy) led to extreme embitterment, and people must have begun to talk when it became clear that the prince, in his father's absence the natural leader of any expedition of this kind, would on no account take part. In the middle of June 1412, according to Walsingham, Henry issued at Coventry a defence of his conduct, excusing himself from the expedition on the rather feeble ground that he was only allowed to take a very small force with him, insufficient for his own security, and protesting in the strongest terms against the slander that he was planning a violent coup d'état with popular support. At the end of the month he paid his father a visit, recorded with the fullest detail by the translator, who makes Henry disguise himself, secure entry to his father's chamber and presenting him with a dagger, ask the sick king to slay him if he was suspected of any treachery or disloyalty. Henry IV then forgives him in an affecting scene.

Walsingham is probably nearer the truth in saying that the prince protested his loyalty and asked permission to prosecute his slanderers; and that Henry IV 'appeared to assent to his pleading', but indicated the next parliament as the

proper place to pursue his detractors. We
know that the detractors were busy in August
1412, when they charged the prince with mal-
administration of the Calais finances, and put his
treasurer in the Tower. If Walsingham is right,
there was every reason for Henry to object to
the policy of the new Council. The French lords
appear to have circulated, as a bait, a number
of unconditional promises, wholly different from
the detailed terms eventually agreed, which
delighted the king and the archbishop. They
offered 'the duchy of Aquitaine entire, as his
predecessors had it, without exception'; they
offered 'their daughters and their nieces in
marriage; their castles, towns treasure and other
goods to do honour to the said lord king'. The
monk of St. Albans may be inventing a little,
but it is clear that a glowing picture of the proposed concessions was presented to Henry IV
and Arundel, and that the proposal was treated
more seriously than it was worth. In 1407 the
prince had seen how much Armagnac help was
worth to Owen Glendower; he had a shrewd
idea that the French lords would not hold to
their word, and, as we know, he was right. The
expedition, led by Thomas, Duke of Clarence,
fizzled out prematurely owing to the reconciliation
of the parties in France, and the English forces
were left in the lurch.

Legend has also played around the prince's
wildness and his sudden conversion at his acces-

sion. The servant of Mars and Venus was 'suddenly changed into a new man'. The gay youngster who could ambush and rob his own receivers or could treat Chief Justice Gascoigne with contempt became a serious and grave king. In his preface, the translator of Livius states that from the time of his father's death until his marriage Henry remained strictly continent. The wilder members of his household he is said to have rebuked and dismissed; in the purge he retained only the four 'which had been full heavy and fain would have him forsake riot', and sent to his grandmother for twelve gentlemen of sad governance. There is no means of checking these statements. It is a good English tradition that the Prince of Wales should enjoy himself, and a medieval household was never easy to control. Popular opinion would naturally expect some pranks from a young man of high vitality and physical charm like Henry; and contemporary moralists would like to feel that his father's death aroused in him the sense of vocation. His chaplain quietly says that at the time of his accession he was 'in age a young man, in maturity an old': *aetate juvenis, maturitate senex*; and that is probably the best description of a prince who had already packed into twenty-six years a unique amount of public duty, and had grown up in the hard school of the Welsh Marches.

He had a striking appearance. The surviving portraits and the description of him by Titus

Livius agree in giving him a long oval face, straight nose, high cheek bones, a deeply indented chin and large expressive hazel eyes. The thick brown hair is cropped above his forehead; the lips are full and red, the neck long, the body active and graceful; a fine runner and jumper, more of an athlete than a statesman. Ardent in temperament, a merry companion (he had a taste for burgundy), he was yet a good listener and a reader. Whether as prince or king, he had in his library, besides the inevitable books on hunting, legends of the Crusade, the works of St. Gregory, Chaucer's Troilus, two poems which Hoccleve and Lydgate wrote for him, and various moral and didactic treatises dedicated to him. Richard Ullerston, Fellow of Queen's College Oxford, at the request of Richard Courtenay, the Oxford Chancellor, sent him between 1404 and 1408 the *De officio militari*, a treatise on the moral and spiritual requirements of a knight's office, wherein he commends Henry for concerning his mind with the scriptures and for his zeal for the house of God 'which is the church and clergy', as well as for having at his side people expert in political and military science: 'and whatever he may lack in philosophical matters, his desire for spiritual study will, God favouring, supply'.

Hear him but reason in divinity,
And, all-admiring with an inward wish,
You would desire the king were made a prelate.

the archbishop is made to say (*Henry V*, Act 1, Sc. i). Ullerston has put it with less exaggeration. The 'desire for spiritual study' may have prompted his choice of confessors, the brilliant Oxford Carmelite Stephen Patrington, a leading opponent of the Lollards and an academic teacher of high standing, and, after his death in 1417, Thomas Netter of Walden, who at his request wrote the *Doctrinale*, a defence of the Catholic faith against Wyclif: a Carmelite also, successor to Patrington as provincial of the order, equally passionate against heresy. As dean of his chapel Henry chose Robert Gilbert, later dean of York, and (1436) bishop of London, a distinguished scholar who spoke for the universities in the Canterbury Convocation of 1417. Gilbert was a clerk with a conscience, as is shown by a petition to the Pope in 1435, when he asked for a dispensation on account of irregularity. Twenty years before, he said, he had gone to France with Henry V as dean of the king's chapel, and had been several times present in battles; and while he had killed and wounded nobody, he was troubled in conscience because he rejoiced when the king's forces had the victory and lamented when they were beaten. . . .

Henry can be judged by his appointments. While it was for the Papacy to provide to English bishoprics, it was for the king, usually after discussion with the council, to make the appropriate suggestion; and, generally speaking, Henry

C.2

got the prelates he asked for, sooner or later. Distinction of mind and character he valued more than administrative ability or courtly compliance. Only two 'king's clerks' (i.e. professional civil servants) secured promotion: John Wakering (Norwich), like Bubwith of Bath and Wells formerly a Chancery official, and John Chaundler (Salisbury) who to his credit spent most of his later days, whether as dean or as bishop, in the cathedral whose singing he loved, a generous benefactor of its vicars choral. Henry Ware (Chichester) a Welshman who had been a valuable diplomatic negotiator, had, it is true, been keeper of the privy seal, but his appointment to that office had come as a surprise, the chaplain tells us, and he cannot have possessed the official mind. Of the others, two rose through their knowledge of canon law and curial procedure; John Kemp, whose upward course ended in Canterbury, had been dean of the Arches, and Thomas Polton (Hereford—Chichester— Worcester) a great figure in the court of Rome. The majority were distinguished scholars like Patrington himself (St. David's—Chichester), William Barrow (Bangor—Carlisle), Roger Whelpdale (Carlisle), provost of Queen's College, Oxford, Richard Fleming (Lincoln), founder of Lincoln College, or Richard Courtenay (Norwich), to whom Henry was devoted, 'the king himself closing his eyes', says the chaplain, on his death-bed in camp at Harfleur.

The most significant choice was Henry Chichele, bishop of St. David's, for Canterbury (1414). Chichele was the man who combined high academic power with great practical experience, and already knew the mechanism of church and state to an extent only shared by Thomas Langley of Durham, the greatest church figure in the north. Chichele had been with the notable reforming bishop, Robert Hallum of Salisbury, at the Council of Pisa; before that he had been engaged on negotiations for the prince's marriage, and by the time of his promotion he must have been expert in diplomacy with the French. He was anything but a proud prelate; a man of human affections, friendliest disposition, and first-rate practical efficiency; more merciful than Arundel towards Lollards, and all his life a keen upholder of the university and of university graduates in clerical appointments. To represent him as a compliant servant of Henry V is entirely mistaken; it is even possible that the influence operated, moderately and tactfully, the other way.

If we have anticipated a little, it is to show what Henry required from his pastors of *Ecclesia Anglicana*. At the council of Constance clerics like Hallum, Bubwith, Spofford, abbot of St. Mary's York, Stephen Patrington or Henry Abendon, warden of Merton College, could hold their own with any delegation, and Henry maintained this level throughout his reign. His own standard of letters was sufficient: he could write in Latin and in French: but more interesting is his deliberate use of English in his official correspondence. This was noted in 1422 by the Brewers Company when they decided to write their own minutes in the vernacular. On his campaigns he wrote news-letters in English to the mayor and citizens of London, reporting progress to the municipality which had given him such great financial help. From these missives the chroniclers of the city drew information to insert in their all too brief English record of each successive year of the mayors and sheriffs. Normally in writing to a senior abbot of the Benedictine order or to its English presidents a king would use Latin. Henry now, under his signet 'of the eagle', corresponded in English. The writing is direct, straightforward: an English, as Caxton was to say of Chaucer, 'not over rude ne (nor) curyous, but in suche termes as shall be understanden'. In it are the first gleams of nationalism.

In Shakespeare it is the outward change of Prince Henry into Henry V which forms the theme of the latter part of *Henry IV, Part II*. This is necessary to the dramatic structure of the historical plays, where contrasts must heighten the young king's appeal. Inwardly, as the dramatist saw, there was little transformation, save perhaps in dignity, and moderation. The ardour, the strong will remained, now combined with the power to conciliate and stand in a central

41

position. Most significant was to be the faithful devotion of Henry's brothers and relations, especially Thomas Duke of Clarence, with whom he had seldom seen eye to eye. Clarence now put his suspicion of the Beauforts aside. Friction in the council, at any rate for the next six years, disappeared. It was perhaps well, since the dangers were still great. If the crown descended upon Henry

> with better quiet,
> Better opinion, better confirmation,

there were still formidable crises to test the government before the problem of France was ready for solution.

Chapter Three

Threats to the King

IT is characteristic that the chaplain who wrote
the *Gesta Henrici Quinti* should begin his story
with the Lollard attempt to capture the king
and seize the city of London in January 1414.
He says nothing about Henry's first appointments—Henry Beaufort as chancellor, the Earl
of Arundel as treasurer, Sir William Hankford
as Chief Justice of the King's Bench; or of the
first parliament in which the commons voted
Henry the subsidy on wool (43s. 4d.) for four
years as well as the usual tenth and fifteenth; or
of Archbishop Arundel's convocation which similarly granted a tenth. Upon his mind was burnt
the fact that the Christian king, the upholder of
and defender of the church, whose great desire
was to bring to an end the devastating strife of
England and France, was at the very outset
'tried in the furnace of tribulation' by the
treachery of one of his most intimate companions,
Sir John Oldcastle, Lord Cobham.

In Shakespeare there is no word of this.
Though the Southampton plot of 1415 has its
own scene (*Henry V*, Act II, Sc. ii) neither before
nor afterwards is there any hint of the back-

ground of treason and discontent with which
the social historian of the time must reckon.
Apart from that episode, Shakespeare makes the
career of his Henry sunlit and straightforward.
It was not always so. The more obvious public
dangers aside, Henry's own temperament gave
him little rest. He was not exempt from the contemporary fear of necromancy and magic. At
his request the province of Canterbury was
instructed to pray for him against it. Sorcerers
were brought before the King's Bench, and his
own stepmother, Joan of Navarre, was arrested
along with the members of her household and
relegated to seclusion for her suspected share in
magical arts against him. When he lay dying
in France, the black shadow came. " 'Thou liest,"
gasped the king: "my portion is with the Lord
Jesus," as if he were boldly addressing the evil
spirit' (*quasi spiritum malignum audacter alloquendo*),
the chronicler writes. The medieval spiritual life
had this dark background, and Henry, who
knew its exaltations, was conscious also of its
terrors.

Between 1414 and 1417 religious and dynastic
opposition were intertwined. Henry's re-burial of
Richard II at Westminster was not mere piety:
it had the political motive of showing that Richard
was veritably dead, not alive in Scotland with
the Duke of Albany, waiting to oust the Lancastrians. For four years many were to believe
this. In Yorkshire and northern England gener-

ally the death of Archbishop Scrope had not been forgotten; the battle of Bramham Moor in 1408 had been the end of the old Earl of Northumberland, but there were still sympathizers with the Percy cause. In Scotland, many disliking the regency assumed by the Duke of Albany were anxious to recover James I (captured at sea in 1406) and Murdoch of Fife (taken prisoner at Homildon Hill 1402) from their English captivity, and Henry, the day after his father's death, by way of precaution had both men sent to the Tower. The regent himself was no more friendly disposed to England, and the French alliance of the two previous reigns had been renewed. But the immediate danger came from Lollardy which had made rapid strides during the last years of Henry IV's reign. It had acquired a powerful influence among certain knights of the shire, who, while not necessarily practising Lollards themselves, contrasted the poverty of the government with the wealth of the church, and in 1410 put forward the famous petition for the confiscation of clerical temporalities. Walsingham reflects on the 'malice of the parliamentary knights and their extremely disingenuous proposal' i.e. that the confiscations might bring in 332,000 marks to the exchequer, from which the king could maintain a large force of earls, knights and esquires. This petition was formerly doubted by historians, but there is evidence to show that a proposal of the kind was actually made at a time when the government stood badly in need of money.

Lollard doctrine rested on two main foundations, one purely religious, the other ultimately political. The first was the absolute priority of scripture over any and every other authority, whether the teaching of the fathers, the interpretation of the Church, or the definitions and decisions of the see of Rome. Any individual believer who approached the text of scripture with sincerity and humility was competent to interpret it for himself. The Wycliffite translations, the mission of the poor priests and the vernacular writings and sermons of Wyclif himself were all based on this tenet, which was the error countered in Archbishop Arundel's drastic censorship regulations of 1409. Arundel had two aims: that popular exposition of the Bible in English should not be based upon unauthorized translations, particularly on tendentious paraphrase; and (because he very sensibly saw that you could not control what was said in the pulpit) that the preacher or teacher should be properly accredited. Yet for all his efforts, groups and circles of readers were forming themselves in different parts of the country, particularly London and East Anglia (Norwich and Colchester); for there the parchment-makers, the scriveners who copied texts and the limners who illuminated the sheets—the technicians of the book-trade, who catered equally for the orthodox and unorthodox—

were most abundant. Their clients were often comparatively illiterate people who gathered round a clerk or leader of the study circle and listened to the new doctrine. It was at the limners' that were seized the treatises which sent a number of Lollards to their destruction, when the civic authorities began to help the ecclesiastical in their searches for suspected material. Such students and expositors were later called by Bishop Reynold Pecock the 'Bible men' or the 'lay party'; their doctrine, he said, took the form of three 'trowings': the first was that no precept of the moral law is to be esteemed a law of God unless it is founded upon scripture; the second, that every humble-minded Christian can arrive at the true sense of scripture: the meeker he or she is, 'the sooner he or she shall come into the very true and understanding of it, which in Holi Scripture he or sche redith and studieth'; the third, that when the true sense of scripture has been reached, the Christian should listen to no argument of the clergy to the contrary.

The second tenet was derived from the accusations which Wyclif brought against the contemporary church.

His charge against the church of his day was that it had deviated from the true church of Christ and his apostles; and this view, which pervaded Lollardy, was probably derived from the position he had adopted in the classic debate

47

over the nature and implications of lordship (*dominium*) when he insisted that lordship—we should say *ownership*—was only justified if founded upon grace. If grace was the only title to lordship, what could be said of the propertied church (or sect) of the late fourteenth or early fifteenth century or of its leaders, the Pope, the cardinals and the bishops? Wyclif answered the question by denying the church's title to her lands and wealth and all the dignities and attributes of the clergy that were based on long possession and usage. Like him, the Lollards brought the institutional church of their day to the touchstone of moral values: but—and this is the point—the valuer must be the individual believer, the interpreter of scripture in his own right. It was *his* valuation that counted.

When the chaplain observed that Sir John Oldcastle had adopted 'all the heresies which Wyclif under a sophistical new terminology had summoned up from ancient paganism', he was thinking primarily of this denial of the authority of the *Catholica*, which St. Augustine had to face in combating African Donatism with its similar contrast between the 'pure' church of the true believers and the polluted church of the later Roman Empire. Oldcastle himself was a trusted lieutenant of Henry when representing his father in the Welsh Marches. Several times knight of the shire for Herefordshire, his home was at Almeley in that county, an area which

Professor Tait has described as 'a hot-bed of Lollardy'. Ten miles to the north-east, at Sutton Park near Tenbury in Shropshire, lived another formidable Lollard, Sir Roger Acton, who also had lands in Church Stretton and had been sheriff of Shropshire in 1410. Not far off, near the Gloucester border, lived another of the type, Sir John Grendor, a former sheriff of Glamorgan, who had been in the prince's household. All three men, resembling in type the later Cromwellian Ironsides, were veterans of the wars against Owen Glendower, serving their young master from Shrewsbury to Aberystwith, loyal and efficient.

Oldcastle was more than that, for he was of sufficient standing to go with Clarence in a high-command on the French expedition of 1411. His marriage with the widow and heiress of Lord Cobham had brought him to a position of prominence both as a lord summoned to parliament and as owner of considerable estates in Kent. It was impossible to ignore his activities; and the seizing of a highly heretical unbound book belonging to him at a limner's in Paternoster Row in London constituted damning evidence, which was reported to Convocation in March 1413. As he was an important magnate, Arundel referred the case to the king, and for several months Henry, 'having compassion on the knighthood of the said apostate', did his best to convert him. In the end, when Oldcastle proved obdurate and left Windsor, without leave, to shut himself up in Cooling Castle, there was nothing for it but to authorize Arundel to proceed against him. Oldcastle ignored the citations, but in the end submitted, paid another visit to Windsor and was thence conveyed under arrest to the Tower. He was brought before the archbishop in St. Paul's on 23 September, 1413, and given another chance to secure absolution. Instead, he produced a confession of his faith in English, and in spite of warnings declined to modify it in any way. When the court reassembled at the Black Friars, he declared that he would seek absolution from God alone, and becoming abusive, denounced his judges to the spectators as men whose teachings would lead them to hell: whereupon Arundel excommunicated him and handed him over to the secular arm. With great leniency, however, he was given another period for further reflection, and during this stay of execution his friends rescued him from the Tower. For two months he was in the London neighbourhood planning violent action which aimed at capturing the king and his brothers during the Christmas and New Year festivities at Eltham, seizing the city of London and putting to death a number of higher clergy. But Henry, through his agents and spies, got to know of the plans in advance: various Lollards were arrested and gave away the particulars. The London stage of the rising was timed for 9 January, 1414, and on the 8th

Henry quietly moved from Eltham to West-minster. On the 9th he ordered the gates of the city to be closed, and having collected a force under cover of darkness, boldly took up a position in St. Giles's Fields. The rebels had expected that the Londoners would come out to meet them: as they came in scattered parties towards the city, they were not given time to assemble at the rendezvous, but were rounded up by the king's guards and marched off to prison with very little resistance.

Henry had laid his plans to bring the insurgents to justice. Commissioners were immediately appointed to try prisoners brought before them by the Earl Marshal, keeper of the Marshalsey prison, and presumably by keepers of the other London prisons. Those so arrested were the men caught red-handed in St. Giles's Field. They were tried on 11 and 12 January by petty jury and judgment was passed immediately. Most of those condemned were executed on the 13th, either by hanging or by hanging and burning. At least thirty-eight, not a very large number, met their death in this way.

On 11 January commissions of inquiry were issued for twenty-one counties as well as London. The reports of the commissioners had to be returned to the Chancery and those presented by the grand juries were, if the case was made out, sent for trial by the King's Bench—provided, of course, that they could be found. If they could not be discovered, they were put in exigent and eventually outlawed. The returns of the inquest are now in the King's Bench class of Ancient Indictments in the Public Record Office.

From them it is clear that while the general plan of the armed revolt was defective, the preparation made for assembling forces in each county were quite thorough. In each, one or two persons, whether priests or laymen, were responsible for the organization, letting Old-castle's supporters know what time they were expected in London, doling out money to them, arranging for the billeting of those who came from a distance and bribing those who could not be persuaded to rise.

The names of the men presented show a pre-ponderance of artisans—weavers, webbers, smiths, turners; and in the country, graziers, corn-dealers, husbandmen, and so forth, led by their local chaplains. It was a rising of the lower grades of society, the inarticulate people who came to life for a brief flash in 1381. Most significant is the appearance of scriveners, limners, parchmeners—the professionals of the book trade. In Bristol, Northampton and, most of all, in London itself, those who made the books helped to make the rising.

Yet it is not from these returns, suggestive as they are of a rising of those who are just beginning to read and think for themselves, so much as from the record of the trials in the King's Bench that the more important facts emerged: facts often not directly narrated, but to be gleaned, sometimes by inference, from the statements of men turning king's evidence ('approvers' they are called), who charged prominent persons with supporting Oldcastle, and must sometimes have caused some embarrassment by so doing. Much relevant detail did not come to light till nearly six or seven years after the rebellion: some of the stories relate to the time of the Southampton plot, or even to the last years of Oldcastle's life (1417) when he was living in Shropshire and Herefordshire.

Oldcastle, it will be recalled, was sent back to the Tower after his trial by convocation on 21-25 September, 1413. He had been condemned as a heretic, but sentence of death under the Act of 1401 was deferred at the king's request, as the chaplain tells us, 'under hope of inducing the lost sheep to return from the oblique path of error'. The lost sheep escaped from the Tower during the night of 19 October, and there are two accounts of how he did it. In the first, a parchment-maker was incriminated: the second involved more important people, like the Abbot of Shrewsbury. Whatever are the real facts of the rescue, it is clear that people could be got out of prison if sufficient skill or force was applied by local supporters, and that Oldcastle was at large in London from 19 October, 1413 till nearly five weeks after the rebellion, probably in the Clerkenwell district, where the Cobhams had land. The king seems to have suspected this, for some Smithfield constables were rewarded in 1414 for having kept watch for Oldcastle by night, and for having seized Lollard books in the house of a parchment-maker; and John Barton, yeoman of Sir Robert Morley, and others were paid for searching a house in Smithfield belonging to William the parchment-maker, in which Oldcastle had lived.

It seems from the legal evidence that the parchment-makers and scriveners had much to do with getting Oldcastle out of prison and maintaining him after his escape. Besides the Abbot of Shrewsbury, other prominent clerks were involved in Oldcastle's movements. A prisoner in the Marshalsey, one Richard Makerell, told how, when he had been several days in sanctuary at Westminster hiding from his creditors, on the evening of 2 February, 1414— it was the evening that the Duke of Clarence came into the sanctuary 'to look for the said Sir John Oldcastle'—he and others hiding there were approached by the monk archdeacon of Westminster who revealed himself 'in full armour save for his head', and were asked, in return for a substantial sum, to ride with a squire of Sir John Oldcastle, also in sanctuary there, to find his master and escort him to a safe place. 'And he (the archdeacon) told them that within

sixteen days John Oldcastle would be sure of
our lord king and that our king would stand
more in peril of Sir John Oldcastle than Sir
John Oldcastle now stands in peril of the king'.
The militant archdeacon is matched in sympathy
by the Cluniac Prior of Wenlock (the west
country connexion again), who was taken into
the Earl Marshal's custody and had to stand his
trial in the secular court for harbouring Oldcastle
during April 1417, and providing him with
counterfeit coin. An approver, William Carswell
of Witney, deposed to having seen Oldcastle at
Wenlock Priory and to have been offered £10 by
the Prior 'to instruct them (the Prior and his
cellarer) in the whole art of multiplying coin'.
Oldcastle was evidently trying to get money
through an illicit mint in the Priory. The Prior
remained in custody from 18 January to 2
February, 1418, when four gentlemen of Shropshire bailed him out to appear in May. At the
May session of the King's Bench the jury declared
him not guilty, but he was sent back to the Marshalsey 'for certain other causes', and was
finally bound over on the security of his Shropshire friends to come up for judgment if called
upon. With such helpers in the west it can be
understood why Oldcastle remained more than
three years at large after his rebellion.

The veteran Lollard was marked out as one
of the collaborators in the plot of July 1415,
framed for the destruction of the king while he

was at Porchester on the way to Southampton for embarkation to France. From the neighbourhood of Malvern, where he was in hiding, Oldcastle was to summon his forces to aid the leaders of the project, and Walsingham draws attention to the notices affixed by Lollards to Church doors in London during March 1415, pointing out that the time of revenge had come. The old rebel was held in check by Lord Abergavenny who collected the Worcestershire levies at Hanley Castle to the tune of 5,000 archers and fighters. That was enough for Oldcastle, and he withdrew.

None the less the Southampton plot was a serious affair enough without Lollard assistance. The leading conspirators were Richard, Earl of Cambridge, Henry Lord Scrope of Masham (Henry V's treasurer) and Sir Thomas Grey, of Heton, in Northumberland. Family relationships help to explain the texture of the scheme which, in brief, was to bring the pseudo-Richard from Scotland, or if this failed, to take Edmund, Earl of March, son of the man recognized by Richard II as his heir apparent, into Wales and there proclaim him king. By exchanging Murdoch, Earl of Fife, Henry Percy, Hotspur's son, was to be recovered, so as to raise the north, rebellion was to be re-kindled in Wales, and the king and his three brothers were to be assassinated. The Earl of Cambridge, younger brother of Edward, Duke of York, was by his first marriage (to Anne Mortimer) brother-in-law of the Earl of March, whom the conspirators did their utmost to exploit. Thomas Grey of Heton, Constable of Norham Castle, was a cousin of Hotspur and bound up with Percy fortunes; but Henry Lord Scrope is the most difficult to explain in this company, for he was, as the chaplain says, 'scarcely third to anybody in the royal secrets': his treachery shows the instability of the throne. It was probably not, as the same writer states, French pay that seduced these men, but the dynastic grievance which had brought the Percies to Shrewsbury, later had caused the alliance of Northumberland, Mortimer, and Glendower and, with occasional flickerings, was to lie dormant until it flared out in the rise of the Yorkists and the accession of Cambridge's grandson, Edward IV. Whatever the circumstances, the Earl of March revealed the plot to the king on 31 July, 1415. Grey was at once executed; Cambridge and Scrope on 5 August, after they had been condemned by their peers, assembled in strength, at Southampton. Each confessed, appealing to Henry's mercy, but in vain.

The reign of Henry V is so often considered as a period of internal order and peaceful government that the abundant evidence of lawlessness contained in our public records must come as a painful surprise. Brawling and rioting, in which even churchmen took a prominent part, was widespread: the worst centres were the Midlands and Shropshire. Further north the franchises of Tynedale, Ribblesdale and Hexhamshire, where the king's writs did not run, were centres of robbery and murder, and an attempt was made in the Leicester parliament of 1414 to make their lords answerable. While Lollardy was responsible for some of the disorder, much of it arose from the weakness of local authority and the powerlessness of sheriffs and coroners. If churchmen were sometimes responsible for breaches of the peace, they could retort that they were frequently the victims of malicious prosecution for felony, especially for rape, by the laity, and were imprisoned for long periods simply upon delation until they bought themselves out, while the horrible practice of castrating clerks was becoming more prevalent. Laymen were ready to bring their personal feuds into church. The appalling scenes in St. Dunstan's in the City of London on Easter Sunday, 1417, when Lord Lestrange and his household murderously attacked Sir John Trussell and a parishioner who went to his assistance, and blood flowed freely, were not isolated outrages: a priest could be murdered within St. Paul's cemetery, and the archbishop's register has further instances of violence both to the persons of the clergy and to sacred buildings. These are not essential to our present theme: but they serve as a reminder that minds and tempers were undisciplined in

Henry's day, ready to be worked upon by the
ill-disposed, and that an incident which could
easily be dealt with by a local police force today
might in the fifteenth century assume formidable
proportions. Treason and lawlessness were closely
allied.

Such is the background against which Henry's
steadfastness and passion for justice, sense of
order and fundamental sanity were noted by all
contemporaries. After 1417 he was never
seriously threatened. By this time his authority
had grown to such a pitch that no disloyal
movement had any chance against him. His
character, his energy, his all-grasping administrative talent were a by-word, proved and tested
as they had been by his first encounters with
'our adversary of France'.

Chapter Four

Henry V and France

AS prince, Henry had induced the council to support the Duke of Burgundy, and, as we saw, an expedition had been sent, but the return of Archbishop Arundel to power and the dismissal of the prince had reversed this policy in favour of the Armagnacs. The resulting campaign, led by Clarence, in which the Duke of York, the Earl of Salisbury, Thomas Beaufort, and the Earl of Ormonde had taken part, achieved nothing substantial, but showed that it was possible for an English army to march from Cherbourg to Bordeaux practically unopposed. It gave the foremost captains a taste for campaigning in France, and revived in them the war spirit of Edward III's earlier years.

The twenty-eight years truce between England and France was due to end. The new king did not immediately show his hand: but he did two things. He revived the project of his own marriage with the Princess Catherine, daughter of Charles VI; and he cultivated friendly relations (again dangling the possibility of his own marriage) with other powers like Aragon and Portugal, so as to build up a southern basis of

69

alliance against France. From the debates with
the Burgundian envoys it is clear that he had
considerable hopes of John the Fearless, and was
prepared to go to some lengths to secure his
friendship: yet it was not to be the alliance that
Burgundy wanted against the Armagnac leaders,
but one which should bring him to the throne of
France. In other words, he would use the duke,
if that elusive and shifty person could be caught
and tied down to definite and practical terms:
but if that was impossible (and the Burgundian
alliance was not indispensable), he would, nevertheless, go his own way. But what way? The
way of justice (as it was then called) or the way
of force? The former lay through a detailed
negotiated settlement of the English claims upon
France, fortified by Henry's own entry into the
French royal house through marriage. The way
of force was to press his full territorial claims,
to ask for Normandy, Maine, Anjou, and Touraine in addition to the ancient duchy of Aquitaine,
and if these were refused, as they very well
might be, to challenge Charles VI on the ground
of a 'denial of justice', refusal to admit his legal
right, and to attack along the best strategic
lines. It was characteristic of Henry to attempt
both. With some anxiety, the commons, thinking of their pockets, asked him (December 1414)
to make every effort in negotiation before resort-
ing to arms. But preparations had to be made in
case negotiations broke down, and a curious

observer who might have happened to be in London during 1414 would have had no doubt that Henry was determined to come to his right whether by peaceful diplomacy or by force. The hammering and noise in the wharves by the Tower would have given him the true answer.

For the king it was a situation full of possibilities. Charles VI and his court by no means saw eye to eye with the leaders of the Armagnac party, Charles of Orléans, Bernard of Armagnac, the dukes of Bourbon and Berry, the Count of Alençon and the constable, Charles d'Albret. He even accused them of wishing to dethrone him. He was equally suspicious of the Cabochians, the ultra-democratic artisan and shopkeeper party which, led by the butchers and the skinners, had in 1413 taken control of Paris and passed an ordinance submitting the government to the control of elected committees. He knew that Burgundy was always prepared to use these elements against the unpopular administration by posing as a democratic deliverer, and that the Parisians were never to be counted upon while the duke was about. He voiced his fears of popular government in a revealing letter to Henry, which by its revelation of the state of affairs in France must greatly have encouraged the young king.

By the time of its arrival Henry had begun to entertain overtures from Burgundy. Ducal envoys, including the chancellor of Flanders, had conferred with him at Canterbury in June 1413 at the time of the memorial service for Henry IV. In May 1414 a Burgundian delegation visited Leicester, where Henry stayed for parliament and met English plenipotentiaries who included Chichele, bishop of St. David's, since 1407 employed on and off in negotiations for Henry's marriage and well acquainted with the French methods of diplomacy. Terms for an offensive and defensive alliance were discussed. The Burgundian suggestion was that the duke should provide 500 men-at-arms for three months, Henry 500 and 1,000 archers or more for the same period. In the campaign to be jointly undertaken, the lands of the Armagnac leaders were to be distributed between Henry and the duke: Henry was to have territories of Armagnac, d'Albret and the Count of Angoulême for himself, and to share with his brother and ally Burgundy those of the Dukes of Orléans and Bourbon, and of the Counts of Alençon, Eu and Vertus. The duke promised not to make any treaty with the Armagnac leaders without Henry's consent. The English delegation, wanting to clarify the arrangement, asked a number of questions about what would happen if Charles VI intervened to oppose the duke or if Henry was to take a fortress belonging to the French king or make war outside the lands of the duke's enemies upon the domains of Charles VI. The replies given were not very satisfactory, especially upon the latter topic which the envoys declared to have been much discussed: they were unwilling to commit their master on the issue.

To the duke this was obviously to be a private war against his opponents, in which he could get useful help from Henry in return for his own assistance. Henry, on the other hand, objected to the idea of reciprocity underlying the proposals. He was an independent sovereign, determined, if necessary, to go his own way, and while ready to fulfil engagements, not bound to anyone. Furthermore he wanted substantial security that the duke would actually fulfil his engagements. Promises were not enough. The envoys declined to enter into any further obligations for the duke, so the discussions were adjourned to Ypres in August. At the Ypres meeting, when the duke himself was present, the English were still more pointed in their enquiries, and fell to discussing minutely the exact wording of the projected treaty. After settling the question of how the lands of the duke of Berry were to be treated, a problem left over from Leicester, they asked point blank that the definition of the enemy should include Charles VI and the Dauphin: an awkward question for a peer of France. The English delegation had been empowered by Henry to receive the homage of Duke John: it was not given. The duke promised a definite reply at St. Omer in a month's time: the step was so grave, he urged, that a little delay must

be excused; by then he would have issued a
formal defiance to his overlord, the King of
France.

When the time for the St. Omer meeting
arrived (29 September, 1414), the duke had
to admit that he had not sent Charles VI the
letter. He was anxious to wait another six weeks
in view of the fact that on 4 September he
had been forced to make peace with Charles VI
in consequence of the active campaign that had
been waged against him by the French king and
the dauphin, Duke of Guienne. In point of fact,
the French had taken Soissons, Laon, St. Quentin and Péronne, and were threatening Artois
when the duke had been forced to ask his brother
Antoine de Brabant, and his sister, the Countess
of Hainault, to intervene. The dauphin had
agreed to an armistice, and in the ensuing treaty
John had renounced the English alliance and
sworn never to make one without the consent
of Charles VI. Henry might have had cause
for resentment at this desertion, had he not
already at the time himself been negotiating
with Charles, a fact doubtless well known to the
Burgundians. It was now time, therefore, to
press Burgundy for definite and concrete pledges
of his determination to assist Henry, when the
time permitted. Through his envoys the English
king asked for a two-years occupation of the
towns and castles of Boulogne-sur-mer and Hesdin,
to be garrisoned by English troops, and of two

other strongholds. Burgundy, disliking the request, again put off a definite reply, but promised to send an envoy to London either to grant Henry's demand or to offer a suitable equivalent. Once more, promises and evasion of the main issue. That, for the time, was the end of negotiations with the duke; but before Henry's ambassadors left St. Omer, they left no doubt in the minds of the Burgundians that their master intended to claim the French throne.

None the less it was expedient to follow peaceful paths as long as possible, and it would be misleading to represent Henry as a master of duplicity. He had convinced himself by his reading of history and by the archives of his foreign department that his case was overwhelming. He had before him records of the non-fulfilment by the French of the treaties of Paris and Brétigny and minor interim pacts, details of the tedious and protracted negotiations for the settlement of maritime grievances, notes on the difficulties in securing justice at Anglo-French meetings to settle disputes, the promises of the opposing French parties, each of them anxious only to destroy the other and burking the fundamental issue of the monarchy. Fortified by a mass of documentary evidence from the time of Edward I onwards, he was yet sufficiently modern to wish to break with the feudal concepts of suzerainty, overlordship and homage from which all that evidence had ultimately arisen, and seek, in virtue of an irrefragable claim to the French throne, dominion there as freely and fully as he had it in England.

While not abating one jot of this claim, he was ready to approach the French by the 'way' of matrimony, in the fifteenth century the normal diplomatic means of securing an alliance, and, in a house with a medical history like that of Valois, a likely method of succeeding to the French throne. Henry, an extremely eligible bachelor, had already tempted the Portuguese royal house to offer for him, and the proposal for a match with one or the other of Burgundy's daughters was still in the air. It was time now to ask for the Princess Catherine with an extremely large dower as the premium; and at the same time to press for territorial concessions that went back not only to 1300 but to the brightest days of the Angevin Empire, when the whole of Western France, from the Somme to the Pyrenees, was in English hands. There were lawyers at hand to tell him that the disinheriting of John by Philip Augustus was an illegal act, and that the duchy of Normandy, as well as Henry II's other possessions north of the Loire, were unlawfully and 'violently' detained. The chroniclers and biographers always lay stress on the *violentia Gallorum* which separated Henry from his right. Even the inhabitants of Harfleur, when it was captured, are made to lament the habitation 'that was not justly theirs'. So too when Henry parleyed with the men of Rouen at the end of the siege, he told them roundly that it was not their city: it was his own.

Throughout the first half of 1414 contact on these matters was maintained, Duke of Burgundy or no duke. In August 1414 a particularly solemn embassy, headed by the Earl of Salisbury and Bishops Courtenay and Langley came to Paris and was magnificently received. After protesting their master's right to the throne of France, the envoys showed themselves ready to 'come down to other things', and link matrimonial and territorial demands in a proposal for a general settlement between the two countries. They came armed with a good deal of information about the debts still owed for King John's ransom by France, facts already found useful when the French pressed Henry for the repayment of Queen Isabel's dower: they brought with them an authenticated copy of John's admission of liability: it might lend support to the figure they were instructed to ask for Princess Catherine's dower. The English envoys suggested that without prejudice to the dynastic claim, the king of England might be content with absolute lordship over Normandy, Touraine, Maine, Anjou, Brittany, Flanders and the whole of the ancient duchy of Aquitaine. The French wanted to keep the marriage question and the territorial demands apart for the present; but the English envoys saw them as interdependent, and, in view

68

of the French attitude, put up their demands for
territory, for they now claimed half Provence
and the castles and domains of Beaufort and
Nogent, on the ground that the latter had once
belonged to Edmund Crouchback, son of Henry
III, through his marriage with the widow of the
Count of Champagne. The claim to the moiety
of Provence went back even further, as this was
the supposed portion of Eleanor, wife of Henry
III. Edward II and Edward III had both made
the claim without success. The envoys maintained that they could not discuss the marriage
question till the territorial demands and the
matter of King John's ransom had been discussed,
but they suggested that if a suitable reply on the
leading issue was given, Henry might accept
two million crowns as the dower of the Princess
Catherine. The French reply was to offer
substantial territories in the south of France,
in fact the duchy of Aquitaine from the Charente
to the Pyrenees, though they could make no
promise about Provence, as this did not come
under the French king's domains. They asked
for a longer period of delay for the payment of
the balance of John's ransom, as the French king
was at the moment engaged in extending his
possessions (at the expense of Burgundy), but
suggested that for the dower Charles VI would
be willing to pay 600,000 crowns, a higher
sum than usual in such cases. Dr. Wylie exclaims
at the 'amazing docility on the part of a great

and high-spirited nation which could go so far to meet such demands'. It was hardly not a nation: the Armagnac lords were prepared to go to almost any length to upset the schemes of their opponent, the Duke of Burgundy.

Yet under the leadership of the dauphin, now eighteen, these same magnates were gingerly feeling their way towards a rapprochement with John the Fearless. The prospect of an Anglo-French alliance seriously alarmed the duke. In February 1415 we are presented with the curious spectacle of two sets of negotiations, the continuation of the Anglo-French talks of August 1414, and cautious approaches by the dauphin, Berry and the French council towards an entente with Burgundy. After a meeting with the Burgundian envoys at the Louvre on 22 February, the dauphin was able to announce a formal peace with Duke John, and the hazardous and fragile reconciliation was celebrated by a *Te Deum* at Notre Dame, at which the Armagnac princes and Anthony of Brabant, representing the duke, were present. The celebrations cannot have been to the taste of the English envoys, who had arrived on 9 February, headed by Langley and Courtenay as before, but now accompanied by Thomas Beaufort, Earl of Dorset, Lord Grey of Codnor, and, along with others, Henry V's own secretary, Richard Holme. When their case was officially stated (13 March) it was seen to contain certain concessions. The envoys were prepared to consider Henry's marriage with Catherine, apart from questions of territory; they would accept a million and a half crowns for her instead of two millions, as long as Charles VI fitted her out with jewels and dresses. Finally they came down to a million as their last word. On the territorial question the French, as before, declined to admit any of the English claims to rights in France, especially in the duchy of Aquitaine, but they were prepared to surrender those parts of the duchy that had been recovered in the last reign as extinguishing the unpaid portion of King John's ransom, for they were ready to go up to 800,000 crowns for Catherine's dower. It was a reasonable offer, but the English envoys said they had no power to accept it: the French therefore suggested sending an embassy to England for further discussions. On their return the envoys reported no result—*sans aucun exploit reporter de leur ambassade.*

As soon as they had returned, the tennis-ball story began to circulate. This was the rumour that the dauphin had sent, presumably by the returning mission, a tun (i.e. a packing-case) of tennis-balls to Henry, telling him to spend his time with them like a good boy, and not presume to quarrel with a noble nation like the French. That the envoys brought any case from the dauphin back with them is most unlikely, for he never saw or had anything to do with any

71

member of the party. But the legend has a basis. In the account of John Strecche, canon of Kenilworth, it is the French who 'blinded with pride' indiscreetly foretold the English envoys 'that *they would send* Henry, king of the English, since he was a youngster, little balls to play with and soft cushions (*pulvinaria mollia*) to lie upon, until he had grown to manly strength later on'. Strecche's words are *predixerunt quod mitterent*: this is different from the other contemporary accounts, Elmham's *Liber Metricus* and a St. Albans narrative, long erroneously attributed to Otterbourne, which state that the balls were in fact sent; from which sources the English translator of Livius took the story, whence through others it came in time to Shakespeare, who puts into Henry's mouth a caustic forecast of the game he will later play with the dauphin. Strecche, living at Kenilworth where Henry was fond of staying, was a fertile retailer of the more popular kind of gossip that filters out from a royal household. Significantly, the St. Albans writer says that the balls were sent to Kenilworth. Possibly some French official in his cups joked about Henry's youthfulness and suggested some such present in the hearing of Richard Holme or one of the envoys, who on his return told the story at Kenilworth, as an example of French insolence and levity. Neither the chaplain nor the French chroniclers mention it. As Dr. Emmerig pointed out, it is uspiciously like the tale of the dispatch, by Darius to Alexander the Great, of a child's ball-game contained in a gold casket. It must have been a most useful piece of propaganda.

By the time the French embassy reached England (17 June, 1415), a great council had been held (16 April) at which the chancellor, Bishop Beaufort, announced that the king had decided to cross the sea to recover his heritage: all arrangements had been made for the government of England in his absence by the Duke of Bedford and a council, and for safeguarding the Scottish frontier, the Marches of Wales and the district round Calais. Obviously Henry had judged that further negotiations were purely academic, except in so far as they enabled him to hand the French a careful and detailed statement of the fundamental reason why he had decided to defy Charles VI. None the less in outward appearances the embassy was treated with all seriousness, the sessions taking place at Wolvesey, Winchester, in the early days of July. The French were headed, as before, by Guillaume Boisratier, Archbishop of Bourges, 'a pompous and arrogant man', the chaplain most misleadingly calls him. At Wolvesey the French professed themselves ready to add the Limousin to the territory which they had already declared themselves prepared to cede and to give 850,000 crowns instead of the 800,000 of their previous offer.

But it was no good. Henry's memorandum, his final and definitive reply, (written to demonstrate that the French king did not really want peace) was a comprehensive statement of the whole course of the negotiations since March 1413. At every stage, he maintained, his demands had been met by evasion: the English embassies had secured only a small part of what they asked for; and the French negotiators had always ridden off by stating that they lacked the necessary authority. Henry had been prepared to send a special envoy to Paris and to wait another month pending his return; he had offered a fifty years truce under stated conditions, and in the meantime had been ready to defer his full territorial claims, but he had received no encouragement. He now called God, and all powers of heaven and earth to witness that if war broke out, it was not his responsibility, but his cousin's, who refused to do him justice. The document must have been carefully prepared before the conference as much for purposes of record as to enlighten 'our cousin of France'. Henry had an excellent sense of propaganda, and lost no chance of establishing his case; a revealing passage from the chaplain shows that in the midst of his preparations, when he must have been busy with a thousand details, he had time to do some canvassing:

And when he had stopped for a little (on his

way to Winchester-Southampton) at the abbey
of Titchfield, not far from the port of Southampton to await the coming of his army and
to hold meetings of his Privy Council, he caused
to be transcribed under letters and seal of
the Archbishop of Canterbury and with the
subscription of a notary the facts and conven-
tions made long time past between the serene
prince, King Henry IV of England, his father,
and certain of the greater princes of France
over divine right and the conquest of the
Duchy of Aquitaine, from which they had
rashly departed against their oaths, signatures
and seals. And he sent off those transcripts to the
General Council and to the said Sigismund,
the Emperor, and to other catholic princes, to
the effect that all the world might know what
wrongs the duplicity of the French had in-
flicted on him, and that he was being compelled,
unwillingly and involuntarily, to raise his
standard against the rebels. The tenor of
which transcript you will find in another book
among the royal evidences and records.

These were the agreements of 1412, entered
into before the fruitless expedition left England
to assist the Armagnac lords. Henry must have
viewed the transcripts with grim satisfaction.
They would come in very usefully now at the
council of Constance and be noted by the German
delegation. For a moment he had forgotten the

cause of church unity, which he so greatly affected.

'Concealing from all but his most intimate council the direction in which they were to sail, he planned to cross to Normandy to recover first of all (*primitus*) his own duchy, which is his fully by right from the time of William I the Conqueror, though now, as of long time past, it has been withheld from him against God and all justice by the violence of the French'. The chaplain perfectly reflects the king's romantic legalism in presenting as Henry's first and foremost task, the recovery of Normandy, of which John Lackland had been disinherited in 1204. The legality of that decision the king challenged with every fibre of his being. The historical fact of the expansion of the Capetian monarchy meant nothing to him compared with the justice of his own claim. If at the end the union of England and France was his goal, the first objective was neither Aquitaine nor Gascony, but his own inheritance from Duke William. To the Seine he was going, to establish at the mouth of the great waterway a bulwark of English power, as Calais was to the narrow straits. By so doing he would lay the foundations of the reconquest of the duchy, and through the duchy effect the capture of the island home of the kings of France.

Whilst negotiating, Henry had been building up formidable resources. His preparations were

on foot. All the lances were mounted, each normally bringing some two to four horses into the field tended by grooms and pages. An English army crossing the channel was therefore similar to a large unmechanized cavalry regiment, or numbers of regiments, borne not in a few great transports, but—since few vessels exceeded 500 tons—in a host of vessels which had to be collected both by impressment and by agreement with the master mariners of the ports—Devon and Cornwall, the Cinque Ports, East Anglia and the Humber estuary. In addition Henry got large numbers of craft from Holland. The appearance of such a force nearing land must have resembled that of a modern amphibious operation without the air support. In addition to the lances and the archers, there was a striking assemblage of specialists, most of them at the king's headquarters. Prominent among them were the four master gunners (all Dutchmen) and their teams, the miners under the command of Sir John Greyndon, the smiths, painters, armourers, tentmakers, fletchers and bowyers, while with headquarters came also the 'tradesmen', masons, farriers, cordeners, turners and carpenters, and the smiths and carters who brought the iron and timber. Most accounts of Henry's campaigns omit the technicians, but Henry was a master of military detail and technique, and had he lived in modern times, would have used the scientist and employed mechanisation to the utmost. His

belief was always in skill rather than in numbers:
but in any case the force was expensive enough,
to say nothing of his large household with the
yeoman of the bodyguard and the clerical staff
attached to the various departments, wardrobe,
kitchen, poultry, scullery, bakehouse and hall;
the king's physician and his archers, the chaplains
and the clerks of the king's chapel, who, when
not singing divine office, were engaged in
secretarial duties; and the eighteen minstrels,
mainly trumpeters, pipers and one 'fiddler',
who were paid 12d. each a day. Prominent
too, as their duties demanded, were the three
heralds, Leicester, Guienne and Ireland, for a
military expedition was a supreme heraldic
event, involving questions of precedence in
station, particularly at sieges, the recognition of
the chief captains of the opposing forces, formal
challenges to the enemy, and the proper reception
of representatives coming to surrender.

The naval preparations were greater than has
sometimes been thought, since Henry had not
only to transport his troops, but also to keep
the sea clear from Plymouth to the Isle of Wight
and from Orford Ness to Berwick. Four large
ships of 120 tons each and ten barges of 100 tons
(each ship or barge carrying forty-eight sailors,
twenty-six men at arms and twenty archers) and
ten balingers (each manned by forty sailors and
ten archers) were required for the latter purpose.
Most of the transport vessels in the 1415 expedi-

tion were chartered or hired: Henry had not yet
built the vessels which he was to use on the second
expedition. These were largely constructed by
the contractor William Soper of Southampton,
and their building shows what Henry was
aiming at. His plan was to discard the galley
and build large sailing-ships of from 400 to 800
tons. This meant wide sail area and two masts,
even three or four being found by the end of
the century. These vessels were built on the
model of the broad, deep cargo ships. Soper's
accounts have in large part survived, and await
analysis from the naval historian.

The army was raised not by the feudal levy
or by the old method of a levée en masse but by
the system of indentures: each captain, whether
of noble or knightly grade, undertook to provide
so many lances and archers for a stated period.
Generally he was asked to provide the first instal-
ment of wages, receiving security and pledges
for ultimate repayment by the exchequer.
His men were required to show themselves
fully armed at the day and place fixed by the
king, who undertook no responsibility for payment until their names had been read and
individuals identified at a muster (*monstratio*) by
officials of the exchequer. As soon as the muster
was passed, the payment of troops by the
exchequer, which had all the lists, could begin.
As payment, the scale per diem was: for dukes
13s. 4d.; earls 6s. 8d.; barons 4s.; knights 2s.;

squires or men-at-arms 1s., and archers 6d. The specialists and tradesmen received 1s. or 6d. There was in addition the *regardum* or reward, a sort of minor bonus for so much service performed, at the rate of 100 marks per quarter for every thirty men employed. There were also 'winnings of war': the ransoms of all prisoners were at the disposal of their actual captors, who generally got a fraction, normally amounting to a ninth, the rest going to the man's captain and a proportion to the captain's overlord. The chief value of a prisoner lay in his ransom. After Harfleur, Henry divided up the chief prisoners among his nobles and the rate of redemption for each was fixed according to rank. The captain of Harfleur, the Sire de Gaucort, had a particularly bad time. Henry forced him to recover some of the royal jewels lost at Agincourt and buy for him 200 casks of Beaune, for which he received no payment: he was not released till after the king's death, when Sir John Cornwall insisted on receiving 10,000 crowns for him and not letting him go until a similar sum had been paid for the Seigneur D'Estouteville, Gaucort having meanwhile to return to France on parole to raise the money.

Certain accounts for the Duke of Clarence's force have survived. He had 240 lances and 720 archers, the largest retinue brought by any noble. His total wage bill was £31 18s. a day and a 9s. 7d. bonus; £223 6s. plus £40 5s.

bonus a week, and £893 4s. plus £161 bonus a month. This is on a higher scale than naval expenses, as is shown by a surviving account of the admiral who, between 24 January and 1 November, 1415 (1 quarter and 39 days) was allowed £1,631 15s. distributed thus: to the admiral for the wages of fifty men-at-arms a day, at 12d., and 150 archers at 6d. a day, £812 10s.; and for the wages of four masters at 6d. a day and 250 sailors at 3d. a day, for four ships, £819 5s. It appears that sixty-five seamen were necessary for each vessel. In 1417 the masters of the king's ships were being paid annuities: in the case of big ships like the Royal Trinity and the Carracks, £6 13s. 4d.; in the case of smaller vessels (niefs) and of the balingers, 66s. 8d.

To pay these forces, loans were necessary. The normal practice of a government under these conditions was to borrow and then repay from taxation, the customs and other sources; and when large sums were asked for, security was given for repayment. The king's crowns, his jewels, precious silver ornaments and utensils, the embroidered vestments and even the reliquaries of his chapel were pledged to individuals or groups of lenders (e.g. municipalities or counties) pending repayment, and many of the picturesque and valuable objects so pawned were not redeemed till well into Henry VI's reign. There need be no surprise at this, for it had become quite a familiar business, though not on quite such a large scale, for it now acquired an office of its own, under the direction of the Duke of Bedford and Bishops Beaufort and Courtenay. Henry sent travelling commissioners all over the country to tap every source of supply and between 1415 and 1417, large sums were raised. Some loan totals for the whole reign may be of interest [1] : the county gentry lent £16,767 6s. 2d., of which £1,140 only was not repaid; the burgesses £6,786 13s. 4d. with £115 6s. 8d. not repaid: the bishops £44,243 (of which Beaufort of Winchester provided the immense sum of £35,630), being repaid all but £2,000; the religious orders £8,758 6s. 9d., with £1,178 10s. not repaid; the city of London £32,096 13s. 4d. with £346 13s. 4d. not repaid. It is interesting to see how liberally the civil service lent: the staff of the exchequer advanced £2,474 6s. 9d. of which only £65 15s. 3d. was unrecoverable: the chancery £1,604 12s. The contribution of aliens was comparatively small: Venetian, Florentine and Lucca merchants put up no more than £3,133 6s. 8d.; but they got rather less than two-thirds back.

The commissioners did their work thoroughly: in Lincolnshire, the classical instance of a county of small freeholders, they seem to have canvassed

1 Mr. A. B. Steel has kindly shown me his detailed lists for the reign, certain items from which he permits me to quote here (cf. his article, "English Governmental Finance" *Eng. Hist. Rev.* li, 29-51, 577-97).

every wapentake and roped in a great quantity of small farmers and yeomen, not merely the sort of people who would be found among the 'lances' of the Agincourt roll, but the archer grades, the kinsmen of the soldiers who in *Henry V* argued with the king on the night of Agincourt. The force that was to accompany Henry to France was not a body of mercenaries, the mixed bands that fought with distinguished condottiere, but one drawn from the country villages and market towns of England, with a sprinkling of Welshmen: independent folk, probably as quarrelsome as Nym and Bardolph; often, but by no means invariably following their own lord; stouthearted, but needing the discipline which Henry was to mete out to them and that mixture of firmness and humanity which has always been the mark of the good English regimental officer.

The total force has been calculated at 2,000 men-at-arms and upwards of 6,000 archers, more than half the latter mounted. Headquarters and specialist units may have brought the total to about 9,000. To carry this, 1,500 ships were required, and it took three days to assemble them along the creeks, inlets and harbours from Gosport to Southampton. Henry's own ship, *The Trinity Royal*, lay in the Solent ready to signal the fleet, when the king was aboard, to make ready for departure. He embarked on 7 August, and on Sunday the 11th the fleet set sail.

Chapter Five

Harfleur and Agincourt

IT was perhaps no mere chance that Bishops
Langley and Courtenay, on their return from
the Paris embassy in August 1414, went down
the Seine by boat and embarked at Harfleur.
The establishment of a strong English base
guarding the mouth of the river and capable of
handling supplies must long have been in
Henry's mind. Harfleur was 'the principal key
to France', and Henry was determined to turn it
into another Calais. It was, therefore, the first
objective of the expedition which set sail from
the Solent with an escort of swans (the chaplain
noted) on Sunday, 11 August, and anchored
off the Chef de Caux in the Seine estuary on the
morning of the 13th. On the 14th, after a preliminary reconnaissance, the whole force went
ashore in small boats and barges, to find defensive
earthworks, but nobody manning them. From
Saint-Addresse, the first camp, the army moved
to the high ground near Graville, about four
km. west of Harfleur (17 August). By the
19th the place was surrounded. The inhabitants
flooded the fields to the north of the town, but
Clarence was sent by a circuitous route to the

far side, not before the Sire de Gaucort had entered to take command on instructions from the French king. Gaucort brought 300 lances to add to the 100 men-at-arms already in the town.

It was not a large defending force, but the place was extremely strong. Situated at the junction of the Lézarde with the Seine, its harbour, strongly protected, was negotiable only at high tide, when the water ran in to a considerable distance. It had a strong curtain of towers and battlements, the whole enceinte was protected by ditches, and outside the main gates, strong points or 'bulwarks' had been constructed from turf, tree trunks and fascines. The problem was to get the guns sufficiently close so as to weaken and blow in the walls, particularly in view of the water surrounding the town. The usual siege equipment of mobile towers could not be applied unless the dykes were filled up, and the jutting-out emplacements offered good cover for the defenders. All gun positions constructed near the walls could be brought under constant fire from the defenders and it was necessary to build cover for the engineers and carpenters making them. The assailants had recourse to mining and throwing forward saps from which the defending strong points could first be overcome, before any general assault was possible. This constituted the first stage of the siege, and it took time because of the difficulty of protecting

87

the men digging. The shooting of the defence was accurate, and counter-attacks were constantly being made. As soon as the strong points had been overpowered and the ditches filled up with hurdles and brushwood, the more intensive part of the siege could begin. But it was a bitter struggle. Only the destruction of the enemy's principal bulwark made this possible, so that large cannon could be brought up to make breaches in the walls; and then it took more than a few days' pounding to blow them in. It was not till 18 September that Henry's major effort could be made and the besieged forced to offer their surrender if no help came. The king had been too optimistic. His miners had not come up to expectations; he had found cover a baffling problem, and the flooding to the north and east of the town had made co-operation with Clarence's forces very difficult.

Worst of all were losses from sickness. The atmosphere of the swampy Lézarde valley in the torrid late summer and autumn and the medieval English soldier's habit of eating quantities of unripe fruit and drinking bad water or overdrinking the local wine were responsible for a bad outbreak of dysentery, through which Henry lost his favourite companion, Bishop Courtenay of Norwich, the young Earl of Suffolk, Michael de la Pole, eight knights, including William Butler, lord of the manor of Warrington, and (later) John Phelip of Kidderminster, as well as 2,000 precious rank and file. It was during the last fortnight of the siege that the mortality increased. On 3 September Henry wrote to the city council of Bordeaux asking for guns and wine, with the cheerful forecast that eight days more would finish the business and enable him to move on to Montivilliers and Dieppe to Rouen and Paris, and then march down to Bordeaux in triumph. All through the siege the king was at the height of activity, sleeping but little, supervising in person every effort of his specialist troops, the most energetic man in the army: but even he had to recognize, by the middle of September, that his resources for a longer campaign were inadequate and that there was no chance of reaching either Paris or Bordeaux. Too large a part of the force had died or had had to be sent back ill to Southampton: the Dukes of Clarence and Norfolk, the Earls of March and Arundel were obliged to return in this way.

The immediate question was how to treat Harfleur, as soon as cannonading and starvation had done their work. When the garrison sent to inquire about terms, Henry was at first disinclined to treat with the negotiators; but in the end he despatched a party, accompanied by the Bishop of Bangor carrying the Host, to parley with Gaucort, as a result of which the town provided twenty-four hostages, and an agreement was reached for the place to surrender if no assistance from the dauphin and the constable of France arrived before 22 September. But the dauphin's countermeasures were leisurely, and Burgundy, though also summoned to help, could not be induced to move. The French army stood fast at Rouen. On 22 September Henry received the garrison of Harfleur at an impressive ceremony. For long he left them waiting on their knees before he consented to receive their submission: then after supping them well he divided them up, as prisoners, among his captains for eventual ransom. The royal standard and the flag of St. George were fixed to the gates and the French flags hauled down; and the Earl of Dorset was made captain of the town. The next day Henry entered Harfleur barefoot to give thanks at the parish church of St. Martin, after which he made his dispositions: there was to be no looting or plundering; all willing to take the oath of allegiance to him were allowed to retain their goods and possessions; burgesses unwilling to submit were to be sent to England until ransomed, while priests and churchmen were allowed to go free. Two thousand of the poorer residents along with the women and children were sent under guard up the right bank of the Seine to Lillebonne, where they were met by Marshal Boucicaut, who sent them in boats to Rouen. They left, says the chaplain, in tears and lamentation at having lost their wonted habitation, 'though it was not rightly theirs': the same note is found in Henry's attitude to Gaucort and his retinue who, in being spared, were reminded that 'against God and all justice' they had withheld from him his own town 'a noble portion of his inheritance'. The evacuation was necessitated by Henry's design to people the place with English; for on 5 October he directed that a proclamation should be made in London and other large towns offering free lodgings and special privileges to any Englishman settling there. During the early winter months it was re-provisioned with victuals from England, while stonemasons and other workmen were sent over to repair the damage done by the siege.

Dysentery had been raging in the town as well as outside, and it was not safe to remain. Henry had to decide what to do. He had only 900 men-at-arms and between 4,000 and 5,000 archers, not counting pages and other serving men. 1,200 had been detailed to form the new garrison, the rest of his force were casualties in one form or another. Despite all the preparations of 1414-15 he had captured only one fortress and lost nearly a third of his army. Instructions to Gaucort that the sixty knights and 200 gentlemen of Normandy set free on parole should deliver themselves up 'as faithful captives' at Calais by November 11, revealed the king's destination. He would march through Upper Normandy and re-embark at the great English port. He would see, says Livius, the country that he claimed as his own. Though his commanders reminded him that he would run into an area where the mounting forces of the French might enclose him 'like sheep in the pens', he would not listen: but he waited a week to see if Guienne Herald would return with the dauphin's acceptance of a challenge to single combat, to decide the issue of the long controversy over his claim to the French throne. The challenge, as it was worded, proposed to leave Charles VI in possession of the crown during his lifetime: if Henry was victorious, it was to be immediately rendered to him upon Charles's decease. This is the first instance of the line which Henry was to take in the Treaty of Troyes; and in the challenge too the dominant idea in Henry's mind outweighing all other conquests suddenly breaks forth.

For it is better for us, cousin, to decide this war for ever between our two persons than to suffer the unbelievers by means of our quarrels to destroy Christianity, our Holy Mother the Church to remain in division, and the people of God to destroy one another.

This is not a pious flourish. Christendom must heal its divisions, political and religious, and with its nations peacefully united under a single Vicar of Christ hurl back the infidel from the Holy Places; the union of the two kingdoms of England and France was to be the political, the union of the church the religious, preparation.

No answer was received from the dauphin, and the English force started on 6 or 7 October (the date is uncertain) its march of 150 supposed miles to Calais—'a way of eight days' the chaplain hopefully remarks: which for medieval infantry is good going and only to be attempted by an army moving light. The baggage waggons and all stores were left behind; even the coffers containing one of the crowns, a sword of state, various jewels and the Chancery seals were loaded on to pack horses. It is perhaps an exaggeration to call this march, as Dr. Wylie does, 'the most foolhardy and reckless adventure that ever an unreasoning pietist devised'. If the French never showed themselves all the time that Henry was besieging Harfleur, there was a reasonable chance of his getting through to Calais without having to fight, always provided that the crossing of the Somme by the ford at Blanque-Taque was feasible. Henry had not neglected this point. He had arranged for a party from the English garrison at Calais to guard the ford: unluckily the numbers sent were far too small, and the force was driven back before it reached the Somme. In the precious days when he was waiting for the dauphin's answer Henry might have sent a strong advance guard to the southern bank to stop the destruction of the causeways, or at least to reconnoitre, but evidently he was content to leave the matter to the captain of Calais, without satisfying himself personally that things were all right. For that omission he was to pay dearly.

Keeping to the coast, he marched as fast as his debilitated army would let him. His men were in three brigades: the van was under Sir John Cornwall and Gilbert Umfraville, Lord of Redesdale, probably the ablest, certainly the most attractive, of all Henry's younger commanders. In the middle came the king with Humphrey of Gloucester, John Holland and Lord Roos; the Duke of York and the Earl of Oxford brought up the rear. Very soon they met opposition and, more serious, found 'scorched earth'. Passing just to the west of Montivilliers they marched on Fécamp, where a force had gathered to oppose him, but collision was avoided by passing the town on the east. On 11 October they were before the castle of Arques with the harbour of Dieppe some four miles away to their left. Here they were shot at from the walls, but the threat to fire the town unless they were given free passage induced the garrison to let them pass and supply them with bread and wine. On 12 October they were twenty miles on and just south of Eu near the mouth of the Bresle, where a large force was waiting for them, but the leading enemy elements were driven back and the same threat as at Arques was successful: food and wine were provided, and after a brief halt the army marched

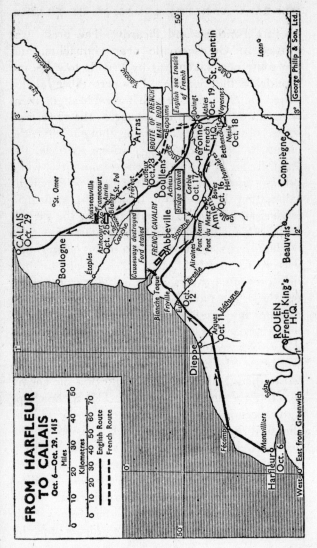

FROM HARFLEUR TO CALAIS
Oct. 6—Oct. 29, 1415

Miles
0 · 10 · 20 · 30 · 40 · 50
Kilometres
0 · 10 · 20 · 30 · 40 · 50 · 60 · 70

———— English Route
– – – – French Route

CALAIS
Oct. 29

Boulogne

Étaples

Ruisseauville
Tramecourt
Azincourt
Oct. 25 Blangy
Anvin
St. Pol
Frévent

St. Omer

Arras

ROUTE OF FRENCH MAIN BODY

Lucheux
Oct. 23
Doullens

Bapaume

English see tracks of French

St. Quentin

Loon

Doingt
Athies
Péronne Oct. 19
French Voyennes
H.Q.
Oct. 18
Nesle
Béthencourt

Acheux
Bridge broken

FRENCH CAVALRY

Causeways destroyed
Ford staked

Abbeville

Corbie
Oct. 17
Corbie

Boves
Amiens Oct. 16 Harbonnières
Oct. 15 Pont du Metz Hangest

Pont Remy
Airaines
Eu
Oct.
12
Bresle

Blanche Taque
Friville
Eu

Compiègne

Beauvais

Somme

Béthune

Arques
Oct. 11

Dieppe

ROUEN
French King's
H.Q.

crête

Fécamp

Montvilliers

Harfleur
Oct. 6

West 0° East from Greenwich

George Philip & Son, Ltd.

95

on into Ponthieu and Picardy. The Bresle was crossed at Gousseauville near Gamaches, and the route now taken was by Friville towards the mouth of the Somme. Prisoners taken at Eu stated that a large French force ahead of them was ready to block the passage to the river, and some, observes the chaplain, thought that the enemy would never be so spiritless as to let the English get any further with impunity, while others (and probably Henry himself) maintained that the dissensions between the Armagnac leaders and Burgundy would prevent the French forces advancing into Burgundian territory.

Henry was right—up to a point. Burgundy was not in the field, but suspicion of him had not prevented Marshal Boucicaut from being on the right bank of the Somme, waiting to dispute any English crossing, and when Henry was approaching the low-water ford of Blanque-Taque, his scouts and cavalry patrols sent back word that 'the bridges and the causeways' which led to them had been broken and that the enemy was in force on the other side. This is the chaplain's version, and another account has it that the ford had been staked, while 6,000 of the enemy were waiting on the far bank. With a boggy river like the Somme it would have been quite enough to destroy the causeways leading through the marshy swamps to the actual crossing place. Henry therefore, to the dismay of his troops, had to seek a passage higher up the river. Rations were running out, the men were tired, and the prospect of meeting the main body of the French another sixty miles or so upstream 'at the source of the river' was not encouraging. And so began the disheartening march up the Somme, with the enemy shadowing them on the other side: past Airaines and Picquigny, with a wide détour south of Amiens, to Boves (where Henry had to stop the thirsty troops from drinking too deeply from the wine vats); then on despairingly to Nesle, where the inhabitants, in order to get rid of the invaders, indicated two possible fords at the villages of Béthencourt and Voyennes, each approached by a causeway. It so happened that the guarding of these had been entrusted to the men of St. Quentin, who, expecting that Henry would try to get across higher up, were not in sufficient strength to stop him repairing the broken parts of the causeways with doors and other material seized from neighbouring houses. This done, it was possible to wade or swim across the Somme, and by the evening of 19 October the whole force was safely over and moving on to Athies and Monchy-Lagache five or six miles south of Péronne.

The same day, 19 October, the French commanders decided to bring the English force to battle. Leaving the king, the dauphin and the Duke of Berry behind, the army had already started from Rouen, and passed through Amiens to Péronne. At Péronne tidings of the crossing had provoked the decision. There was some disagreement, for the constable (d'Albret) and Marshal Boucicaut both advised leaving the English to escape to Calais, as a fight with a desperate enemy was needlessly costly, and it would be quite sufficient to besiege Harfleur. But at the advice of the Dukes of Orléans and Bourbon this plan was rejected, and it was decided to send Henry a formal challenge by three heralds. (The engaging figure of Mountjoy in *Henry V* is a fabrication derived from the Mountjoy King-at-arms mentioned by Hall. No such person was at Péronne, nor was he sent from Rouen by the king, as *Henry V*, Act III, Sc. ii states). The heralds found and told Henry (20 October) that the French would fight him some time before he reached Calais, but 'assigned no day or place'.

The king received the news with calm assurance [1], told the army and made his plans for battle the next day. On the morrow (22 October) no enemy force was encountered, but in the neighbourhood of Péronne the English saw the tracks of a vast French host crossing their line of march, a disquieting reminder of what was in store. Henry passed unmolested over the Ancre at Miraumont, then through

---

[1] 'Benignly receiving the grace of God' says the Chaplain (*Gesta Henrici Quinti*, p. 48): not 'with delight' as Wylie suggests (*Henry V*, ii, 126).

Forceville, Acheux and Beauquesne; then over
the Grouche past Lucheux to Bonnières, till on
23 October the vanguard reached Blangy on
the Ternoise. A fortnight earlier a single reconnaissance plane, had such mechanisms existed,
might have given Henry all the information he
needed about the Somme fords and bridges; so
now it would have told him that for three days
his own and the French army had been marching
north-eastwards close to one another, the French
ahead and half right. Neither force knew the
whereabouts of the other; the French followed
the right bank of the Ternoise to Anvin, when
on 24 October they were detected by Henry's
scouts; the English main body saw them when it
had crossed the Ternoise at Blangy and mounted
the hill on the other side. There they were,
three miles ahead, emerging from the valley on
their right, in three huge contingents 'filling a
wide area (Agincourt to Ruisseauville) like an
innumerable number of locusts'.

The chances of Henry cutting his way through
seemed small: but the king made his battle dispositions, and his halted troops were first confessed by the priests of his chapel. The position
was pretty desperate. The road to Calais passed
through the triangle formed by the woods of
Agincourt to the north-west and Tramecourt to
the north-east, and the village of Maisoncelles to
the south. On the open ground between the
two woods the French had decided to bring

Henry to battle, and there was no escape. He made a last effort to get clear away by sending over prisoners with terms to the enemy, promising to restore what he had taken and to give security for damage done, if he was allowed to pass. Otherwise he asked that he might have battle next day. He cannot have hoped for acceptance of his terms: what he aimed at was to get a night's rest for his troops, and they needed it badly. Probably it was during these waiting moments that the chaplain heard the celebrated remark of Sir Walter Hungerford (not the Earl of Westmorland, as Shakespeare has it) to the king, wishing that he had 10,000 of the best archers of England 'who would long to be with him'.

To whom the king said: 'You speak foolishly; for by the God of Heaven on whose grace I rely and in whom is my firm hope of victory, I would not have a single man more than I now have. For this people I have here is God's people, and the one which today He thinks it right for me to have. Do you not believe that the Omnipotent can, through this small force of men, conquer this pride of French who boast themselves in their multitude and in their own strength?' As if he were to say, He can, at his pleasure. And in my judgment no evil thing could of true justice happen to the son of such great confidence.

The offer was rejected and the king stood ready. But no onslaught came. At dusk Henry sent his force into the gardens and orchards at Maisoncelles to get what rest they could. Strict silence was enjoined: the only noise in the English camp was the hammering of the armourers making ready; but the French could be heard shouting and calling to one another, and at their headquarters (prisoners must have told this later) the commanders were playing dice for Henry and his lords. All night it rained pitilessly.

Only a leader of great character and disciplinary power could have maintained his troops in a condition to fight after that gruelling Burmese march of sixteen days, when food was scarce, clothes wet with wading and rain, and many, as they reached the cold uplands of Picardy, were suffering from a recurrence of that most weakening of diseases contracted at Harfleur.

> Tell the constable,
> We are but warriors of the working day.
> Our gayness and our gilt are all besmirched
> With rainy marching in the painful field.

In his care for the men and his blending of firmness and humanity Henry made a profound impression on his chaplain biographer. The disciplinary orders he issued at Harfleur, later

(1419) at Mantes and Rouen, were, of course, based upon earlier standing orders going back to Richard II's time: the difference was that Henry really enforced them. He forbade the burning of the countryside, except at his express order, the spoliation of churches and church property, attacks on priest and clergy and the violation of women. The English soldier who stole, on the march towards Nesle, a pyx containing the Host (Shakespeare makes it a pax, which is different) was immediately hanged, and a similar fate befell a foreign soldier who stole one from St. Faro's abbey in 1421.

At the fords of Voyennes and Béthencourt he posted himself at one end of the main infantry crossing to prevent overcrowding and ensure that the men went over quietly. He looked jealously after his archers and taught them to protect themselves by the device of the stakes sharpened at both ends and planted in the ground before their positions, to form *chevaux de frise*—almost the old drill-book device of the square for savage warfare. He had no use for helter skelter methods: when his troops were approaching Harfleur, he told them not to hurry: 'Fellows, be of good cheer, and take breath and keep cool, and advance quietly, for with the love of God we shall have good tidings'. In so small a force—the best estimate gives the total before Agincourt at 6,000, facing a French army notably superior in size—he could give personal supervision to every detail. If there is no actual authority for Shakespeare's story of the king's moving alone through the camp during that last night before Agincourt, it is perfectly well-founded upon Henry's practice. He went everywhere, saw everything for himself, whatever the hour.

Next morning, the day of Saints Crispin and Crispinian, before action was joined, Henry called up the transport which had already been raided in Maisoncelles [1] — the coffers containing the crown, the jewels and the seals had been stolen — so as to prevent further plundering. The chaplains, mounted, were sent for, too. That was how his clerkly biographer, who otherwise would have been left behind in the village, came to witness the whole fight from his horse 'in the rear of the battle', and faithfully he described it. The only advantages the English possessed were the ground and (in event) the weather. The ground, because by moving forward Henry forced the French to attack him on a frontage narrow enough to protect his flanks and wide enough to let him deploy in three bodies, each consisting of men-at-arms flanked by two wings of archers; the weather, because for nearly a mile in front the ground was miry ploughed fields soaked with the incessant rain and very difficult for

---

[1] It is now established that the plundering of the baggage took place before, and not during the later stages of the battle.

cavalry or heavily-armed foot. The battle began after a long pause in which either side waited for the other to start, with an attempt by two squadrons of French cavalry under the count of Vendôme and the Admiral of France to ride down the English archers. The mud prevented any pace or momentum on the part of the enemy— the screen version of *Henry V* makes them go at a spirited gallop—and the French horsemen were mostly shot down before they reached the archers' stakes.

Meanwhile the first line of the French men-at-arms, unmounted and led by the flower of their force, the Constable, the Dukes of Orléans and Bourbon, the Counts of Eu and Richemont with Marshal Boucicaut, advanced, to be followed after a good interval by a second line under the Dukes of Alençon and Bar. The third French 'battle', well to the rear, retained its horses to be used in pursuit when the English broke. The first line quickly fell into disorder under English arrows, the mud, and the general confusion produced by the returning cavalry. Yet there were enough of them to make their weight felt, and Henry's column in the centre recoiled a short way: but, as Monstrelet pointed out, the French were jammed so tight as not to be able to use their lances, and at this point Henry signalled the archers, who had been shooting from the flanks, to come in with every weapon they possessed, axes, swords and mallets, and roll the heavily-

armed Frenchmen over. The remainder of the
French first line was then forced back upon
the second, which had been moving through the
fields to help their comrades, and this too, after
a fierce struggle in which Humphrey of Gloucester
was wounded, was disposed of like the first. The
chaplain noted that the heavily-armoured French
lay in heaps and that the more lightly equipped
English climbed up upon them (*ascenderunt*) and
cut their throats as they lay. The process of
slaying or taking prisoner lasted 'for two or three
hours'. It was then that Henry, who had been
anxiously watching the third French line, detected movement among the mounted troops, and
seeing an attack developing, led by the Counts
of Marle and Fauquembergues with the aid of
Anthony of Brabant (who had arrived late),
gave his celebrated order to kill the prisoners.
Most accounts of the battle attribute this command to the plundering of the baggage, and
some to a special foray of Brabant on his own;
but the chaplain who, from his horse, watched
the whole action carefully, attributes the slaughter
of the prisoners to Henry's alarm at seeing the
French cavalry preparing to advance in great
numbers, and undoubtedly he was right. Henry
had to make a quick decision to enable his tired
troops to face a new danger. Le Fèvre, who was
with the English forces, grimly tells us that 200
archers were told to do the killing, as the majority
of the English men-at-arms were reluctant to

lose the ransom money which their capture would bring. The cavalry attack did not come to much, and the remnant of the French army dispersed as best it could. Overcrowding in the ranks, too heavy equipment, and English archery had cost them the day.

According to the latest estimate by French historians, which departs substantially from the figures given by the chroniclers, the total English casualties in killed and wounded were between 400 and 500 and the total French some 7,000. What hit the French hardest was the number of high-ranking commanders lost. The killed included the Constable d'Albret, the Dukes of Brabant, Alençon and Bar, the Counts of Nevers, Marle, Vaudémont, Blamont, Grandpré, Roucy and Fauquembergues, and the Admiral of France, Jacques de Châtillon; the prisoners included the Dukes of Orléans and Bourbon, the Counts of Eu, Vendôme, Richemont, and Marshal Boucicaut. To Henry the victory was a token of the divine providence watching over England, a justification, through ordeal by battle, of his purpose in France. In the October parliament Bishop Beaufort could point to a 'trinity of divine judgments' in the successes of Sluys, Poitiers and Agincourt, as establishing the claim of the petitioners against the defendants. To St. George Henry's special gratitude went out, for he was the saint whom the king invoked when he moved forward: 'Avaunt banner, and this day, St. George, thy help!' Convocation, at Henry's request, advanced the status of St. George's day to that of a greater double; it was to be a day on which all servile work ceased and parish churches were to be attended as at Christmas, 'to praise God and most devoutly implore the patronage of the saint and of all the blessed, and most fervently pray for the safety of the king and kingdom'. St. John of Beverley had likewise been very helpful, for, Archbishop Chichele told his clergy, it was credibly reported that on the day of Agincourt, at the time of the conflict, holy oil had exuded from his tomb—a sure sign of his interest in the English victory. The day of his translation (25 October) was also the day of Saints Crispin and Crispinian, and special devotions to the three saints were now prescribed.

Yet what must have most impressed the yelling and cheering crowds that received Henry in London on 23 November, when all the usual city decorations were hastily put up and the choirs dressed as prophets, martyrs and virgins sang their welcoming songs, was not the rain of gold leaves, nor the giants of the city, nor the long file of distinguished captives, but the sober and reserved expression of the king as he rode with a little group of his household through the streets to Westminster, to offer at the Confessor's shrine. The chaplain thought that this grave and quiet mien, unaffected by the applause, indicated that he was acknowledging the Author of his victory. May he, perhaps, have been reflecting on the narrowness of his escape and the need for different tactics next time? If any results of a lasting character were to be obtained, a sustained effort would be necessary and a considerable part of France annexed to serve as a basis for further attack. The most careful plans would have to be laid for the occupation and administration of the conquered territory. It was for these reasons that no immediate return to France was possible. The next occasion must be decisive, if he went at all: and in the meantime it was right to see what renewed diplomacy could do.

Chapter Six

The Emperor Sigismund

THE Anglo-French conflict bore closely upon the chief problem in the church: the Great Schism. Since the double election of 1378, Europe had been divided into two camps supporting one or the other Pope; on the whole, the Schism tended to follow the main diplomatic groupings which were the result of the Hundred Years War, England and her allies recognizing the Roman Pontiff, France and her friends the Avignonese. After the death of Innocent VII England had made some effort to get the question considered by the European powers, but she had been too late, and the election of Gregory XII, whatever his undertakings when elected may have been, had merely perpetuated the Schism. In 1408 England had been converted by the cardinals to the project of a General Council, and the following year had sent representatives to the Council of Pisa. But Pisa had resulted in three Popes, not one, for the Avignonese Pope, the Aragonese Benedict XIII, and the already existing Roman Pontiff, Gregory XII, refused to recognize the newly elected Alexander V, still less his able but highly unsuitable successor,

109

John XXIII. It was to solve the *impasse*, as well as to bring reform to the Church, that the Council of Constance met in 1414. The flight of John XXIII from the Council in March 1415 had led to his deposition: but no successor could be elected until the countries supporting the contending popes not only withdrew their obedience, but also could agree among themselves about the method of electing the indubitable pope. To this end it was above all things, necessary to secure the co-operation of those kingdoms which had been supporting Benedict XIII, and to obtain within the Council itself a sufficiently peaceful atmosphere and the banishment of disturbing national animosities. This was the task which the Emperor Sigismund, Protector of the Council, set himself. As we observed, Henry had been doing some propaganda at Constance, and Sigismund, as one of his letters to Henry V makes clear, had received a copy of Henry's written claim to the French throne, for he said that he understood that Henry's rights had been usurped in France. The Emperor, for his part, was anxious to bring about peace between the two countries, since the struggle affected all Christendom. He was only too correct in detecting its baleful effects in the Council of Constance. Always an optimist, a believer in personal interviews and dramatic appeal, he did not understand the strength and antiquity of the animosities between the two countries, how deeply complicated the long-standing issues were, how stubbornly proof against any sort of eager idealism.

The Emperor's own special plan was for an alliance between England, France and the Empire: Burgundy was out of the picture, for he regarded the rising power of its dukes with suspicion. He first approached Charles VI in February 1414, suggesting a personal interview after he had seen and talked with the French princes at Avignon. The French Council showed little enthusiasm for a conference with Sigismund, and replied that the king and his brothers were busy fighting the Duke of Burgundy: but they suggested that if he came to Paris, they would be pleased to discuss matters with him. Clearly any league with France would have to be made by the usual diplomatic methods, and accordingly an alliance was concluded by envoys at Trino on 25 June, 1414. Sigismund promised then and for ever to be a good and perfect friend to Charles, King of France, his heirs and blood-relations, and on the day of ratification he wrote again to the king, recalling that he was still hoping for a personal meeting.

Support for the Council of Constance and probably assistance against Burgundy was what Sigismund wanted. In the middle of 1414 he began to be interested in the proposed marriage of Henry V and the Princess Catherine. Probably this was at the request of the French, who had asked him to use his good offices with Henry on that behalf, negotiations for the time being having come to a standstill. Sigismund accordingly told Henry that he was arranging to meet the King of France to discuss the marriage, provided that Henry agreed to send representations to the meeting, planned to take place at Verdun. 'What great fruit, what benefits would result to the Church militant if you, the King of France and ourselves united in true friendship, could cultivate an indissoluble alliance! No usurper of the Papacy would then dare to resist the three of us,' he wrote, charmed with the idea of a triple alliance to combat the schism—as well as John the Fearless; for he pictured all three monarchs crusading against Duke John, and the usurper of imperial territory, John's brother, Anthony of Brabant; he even offered Henry V whatever parts of Burgundy Henry could effectively seize and hold. In July 1415, when the English menace was upon them, the French really wanted Sigismund. He was then planning his journey to Nice to negotiate the withdrawal of the Spanish kingdoms from the obedience of Benedict XIII, and the suggestion was made that he should go on to Paris, if Louis of Bavaria was prepared to lend him the money for his journey (for Sigismund seldom had any ready money). Nothing came of the project, but while Sigismund was negotiating with the Aragonese at Perpignan in September, news came of the capture of Harfleur, and the Emperor decided to send envoys to France and to England to propose an armistice. Two went, but without result: for Henry had begun his march to the Somme. After Agincourt Sigismund made efforts to meet Henry at Calais, but the movements of Burgundy frustrated all his plans for the time being. In February 1416 he judged the occasion more favourable, and raised sufficient money for the journey by conferring a dukedom on Amadeus, Count of Savoy. He arrived in Paris on 1 March, 1416 with a company of 800, all wearing the same device, an ash-grey cross with the motto, *Deus omnipotens et misericors*.

The French were looking to him to make Henry moderate his demands. When he arrived in Paris in March 1416 they received him lavishly, to his evident pleasure. Sigismund was determined to enjoy himself in Paris and the reports of a Strasbourg banker, Ulrich Meiger, show him hiring minstrels whom he paid three months salary in advance, and inviting, on one occasion, as many as 600 ladies to dinner. Apart from these bursts of extravagance, the Parisians hated him for his close-fistedness. He made no offering at Notre Dame, and gave the choir-boys nothing; even the sacred relics displayed for him elicited no more than half a franc. He visited the *Parlement* on 16 March and tactlessly attempted to preside at a suit that was being heard, and to deliver judgment. Sigismund found the French Council in two minds about the English negotiations. The Dukes of Berry and Anjou wanted peace; but there was a war party led by Count Bernard of Armagnac, which had been emboldened by the count's success against the English at Valmont; for at the beginning of March 1416, Dorset, captain of Harfleur, in the course of a foraging expedition into Caux, had been cut off from his base and had suffered a good many casualties. Though he had been able to make his way back into the town, the prospects for the English garrison were unfavourable. The Count of Armagnac knew that with an efficient sea blockade and strong French forces guarding the roads, Harfleur would be reduced to a serious plight, and above everything else he was anxious to capture the place and prevent it becoming a second Calais. With this source of division in the French Council, Sigismund saw that he could do but little in Paris, and determined to transfer negotiations to England.

He arrived at Dover on 1 May. From the Butler family comes the story that, as he was about to land, Humphrey of Gloucester, accompanied by a brilliant staff, rode into the sea with drawn sword to deny him access if he proposed to exercise any jurisdiction in England as Emperor. It may be perfectly true, for it is exactly the sort of gesture which Humphrey loved, and Sigismund had already shown in

Paris that he regarded himself as more than an honoured guest. As he approached London his reception became progressively more magnificent: at each stage a more high-ranking dignitary was waiting to receive him. Parliament was kept in session partly that he might see it, partly to ratify any decision that might have sufficiently matured. The Emperor was shown all the sights, given the SS collar which he wore at all public ceremonies afterwards, and installed as a knight of St. George (the Garter), the most exclusive order in Christendom. He had brought with him to England, and had presented to the Knights' Chapel at Windsor, where the installation took place, the heart of the saint. 'At Windsor,' wrote Dr. Wylie in a characteristic passage, 'they had only one of the saint's bones, a piece of his arm and part of his skull, so that his heart was a very welcome present.'

There was, of course, no lack of stage-management: but the negotiations, for which Sigismund had come, were undertaken very seriously. The debates on the French situation began when William Count of Holland, Zealand and Hainault, son-in-law of Duke Philip of Burgundy and father-in-law of the dauphin, arrived at the request of the French Council in England. In the negotiations both French envoys and the French prisoners played a considerable part. Henry's terms were, except in one respect, no less severe than in 1415. While professing his desire for peace, he insisted on being left in possession of Harfleur and neighbourhood, and asked for everything conceded to Edward III in the Treaty of Brétigny. That meant all the south-west of France, but in return he was prepared to waive his claim to the French crown. This was more than the French envoys, who were looking to Sigismund to help them, could promise; but the suggestion was made and evidently somewhat favoured that, pending further negotiations, the town of Harfleur should be put in the joint keeping of Sigismund and the Count of Holland, and that the chief prisoners should be released upon security given for their return, if the conversations broke down.

This sensible plan collapsed before a wave of popular discontent at the prospect of giving up Harfleur: the commons, as a London chronicle says, 'growsed full sore' and the king heard of the fact. All that could be agreed upon was that commissioners should arrange for a three years truce, and that within five weeks from its conclusion the kings of England and France, the Emperor and the Count of Holland should meet on the frontier of the March of Calais. But the count did not intend to keep that particular engagement. On 21 June he left London abruptly in annoyance at Sigismund's refusal to recognize his daughter Jacqueline as the heir to his titles; and before going he appears to have told Henry quite plainly that if the invasion of France was renewed, his forces would be on the opposing side. On 26 June Henry and Sigismund separated, Henry to Southampton, Sigismund to Leeds Castle, in Kent. And before the month was out, English envoys crossed to Paris to continue negotiations.

Unhappily, the French envoys at the negotiations, who were hopeful about this truce and the subsequent meeting of the principals, had reckoned without the Count of Armagnac, who was set upon starving Harfleur into surrender. The majority of the French Council favoured the truce and the further discussions; but the powerful and passionate advocacy of the Constable made a great impression, and in the end the Council decided to parley with the English embassy while at the same time not resolving to discontinue the blockade of the port. This fateful policy, or absence of policy, destroyed all hope of peace, and is sufficient to account for the embittered complaints of *Gallicana duplicitas* in English chroniclers. It must be said on Henry's side that he never anticipated such tactics, and was seriously hoping that the Armagnacs would relinquish the blockade while the further talks were in progress. But the English envoys who went to Beauvais, where the discussions were being held, found that the French were extremely chary of reaching any conclusions (they said, for instance, that they must consult the King of Castile before entering upon the three years truce, as proposed in London), and they complained of insulting treatment and confinement in their lodgings. The unsatisfactory conference ended with an agreement to meet again, at Calais or Boulogne, before 16 August; but long before this Henry had fathomed the intention of the French Council, and Sigismund had discovered, to his bitter disillusionment, that his intervention had been in vain.

In England, as the summer went by, all eyes were turned towards the channel and the saving of Harfleur. Would a relieving English fleet break the Franco-Genoese cordon and reach the starving town before the English garrison capitulated? A violent adverse wind had been blowing for days and Bedford's rescuing squadron found itself cut off from the vessels of the Cinque Ports. Only just in time were the two fleets able to unite off Beachy Head, and sail as fast as they could make it to the mouth of the Seine. It was on the night of 14 August that the king's watchmen on the roof of the palace of Westminster saw the beacons and told Henry that the expedition was crossing. In the early morning of the 15th the king asked for special prayers from the recluse of Westminster, Humphrey of Lambeth, whom he had visited for confession on the night of his father's death, as well as from the religious houses of his own foundation, the Carthusian priory of Sheen and the Bridgetins of Isleworth. It was an eventful day, for not only did Bedford, after a seven hours tussle with a formidable sea-foe, break the cordon and relieve Harfleur, but in the evening before the result was known the King and Emperor sealed at Canterbury their famous treaty of alliance, a document which made a deep impression throughout Europe, especially in the Council of Constance.

In this instrument, evidently drafted when the English ambassadors returned from Beauvais and the tactics of the French were discovered, Sigismund recounts the history of the Anglo-French negotiations from the time when he reached England. All his efforts had been directed to restoring unity in the church, and to that purpose he had striven his utmost to bring France and England together. He had done all he could to persuade Charles VI to accept articles agreed on by himself and the Count of Holland, and had almost persuaded the French Council to adopt them; but the French king, a lover of discord, had rejected them in order that he might destroy the unity of the church, as he had constantly done in the past. Sigismund then turned to the tactics of the French at Perpignan; to French depredations upon the Empire, and to the derisory attitude they adopted towards his attempts to secure Henry V his rights. It was time that these devices should be stopped, and he had therefore made with his brother of England a treaty of perpetual friendship between himself and his successors on the one side, and Henry, his sons, or failing issue, his brothers on the other, to resist attacks from every power and person, saving only the church and the Pope. Merchants and craftsmen of either side were to have free access to the dominions of the other, provided they paid the customary dues and obeyed existing laws; neither party should harbour the traitors or rebels of the other or go to war against the other, save in self-defence, but each would assist the other in recovering his respective rights in France. The treaty was therefore offensive as well as defensive, and Henry understood from it that Sigismund would turn out to help him during 1417. It reversed the agreement of Trino, described above (p. 111), and indeed the Luxemburg tradition of friendship between the Empire and the French court: it was a return to the Edwardian policy of the encirclement of France. But it was only partial encirclement, for in between the March of Calais and the Empire stood Burgundy. It became therefore all the more important for Sigismund to settle accounts with the duke, and for both allies to secure his co-operation in any moves that were to be made against France.

Henry was particularly anxious to secure the help of the wily and elusive Burgundian. It was primarily to this end that a meeting of the Big Three had been arranged at Calais in September. When Henry landed after crossing from Sandwich on 4-6 September, Sigismund, who had preceded him, was waiting for him on the beach. They embraced and passed through the town laughing and jesting together 'as befitted imperial highnesses', Henry to the castle, Sigismund to his inn. A good many notables, including Archbishop Chichele, were already there. With the king went our friend the chaplain, who reports all the details of the visit, though he could not gain admission to the council chamber. Next week French envoys arrived, headed by Gontier Col, Archbishop of Rheims, and though treated with respect, were confined to their lodgings, in retaliation for the treatment given to the English at Beauvais. Their proposals, addressed to Sigismund, were an offer to re-open the marriage question, which Henry had refused to consider as long as the French were besieging Harfleur, and to pay down a large sum in advance. The memorandum, of which the original has perished, may not represent all their offers, but be merely an addition to other and more substantial promises. Whatever these were, Henry did not consider them adequate, and all that could be done was to arrange a truce to last until February 1417, called by Wylie 'a hollow sham', which merely covered Henry's preparations for the winter and left him free to pounce with the return of spring. But the main event was the arrival of the Duke of Burgundy, a visit hedged about with extraordinary precautions for security. John the Fearless and Humphrey of Gloucester met unattended in the bed of the river Aa at low water and passed each into the other's territory, Burgundy to Calais and Gloucester (the hostage) to St. Omer.

The conferences between Henry and Duke John were absolutely secret. The chaplain grumbled at the mysterious colloquies, whose outcome never passed 'beyond the royal breast or the silence of the council.' He reports his belief that the duke, 'like all Frenchmen', will be found a double dealer, an obvious testimony to diplomatic skill which would have evoked the praise of Commines. This time, however, Burgundy went farther than his envoys at Leicester, or his spokesmen in the successive conferences of 1414-15; he declared his change of allegiance from Charles VI to Henry; he promised to do homage to the English king as his sovereign, not immediately, but as soon as Henry had acquired a substantial slice (*notable partie*) of France: in the meantime he would assist by every secret means, and would openly take the field for Henry, if called upon to do so. Meanwhile if he made the usual exception about taking arms against the King of France, it was just for the sake of form, 'feigned for the sake of a greater good' (*dissimulé pour ung plus grant bien*): it had no meaning.

This singular agreement with Duke John at Calais is of primary importance in the invasion of 1417. Did Henry believe that John would keep it? Did he know what John meant by it? He was to find the answer to these questions later. It only remained to say good-bye to Sigismund, who himself had got little or nothing out of the Burgundian duke.

When the two monarchs parted 'there was no secret, however mystical, between them', the chaplain says: 'nor, praise God, do people as a whole believe that there was ever greater confidence or affection between two Christian princes.' Henry's spell always worked—his utter confidence in the justice of his case, his skill in presenting it, his fine courtesy, his patience under provocation. And Sigismund's idealism and labours for the universal church, the width of his horizons, his passion for the peace of Christendom were not lost upon Henry. In England, for some reason that is not known, the Emperor's open-handedness contrasted favourably with the parsimony he displayed in France. When he left the country his retinue distributed complimentary broadsheets calling England 'happy and blessed' (*felix et benedicta*); and he took care that the king's household (the chaplain not excepted) were well rewarded for the way they had looked after his comfort. Curiously enough, he still regarded himself as a mediator, morally unaffected by the Treaty of Canterbury. He could not understand the resentment which his action had aroused in France, as the news leaked through; nor did he foresee its effect in the diplomatic circles of the council of Constance, where the embittered French nation drew closer to the Italians and the newly-incorporated representatives of the Spanish kingdom. If the unity of Christendom was his aim, nothing could have been more ill-judged; for at Constance the immediate outcome of the Treaty was the formation of an Anglo-German axis, each nation receiving instructions from its monarch to vote in the council as the other. Quickly therefore, the Latin bloc gathered strength as a retort to the new combination; and Sigismund, on his return, was to find that his old authority over the assembly had disappeared.

Chapter Seven

The Second Invasion

THE chaplain, before ending his narrative of Henry's first three years as king, comments on his master's 'unshakeable decision to cross the Channel the following summer in order to break the obstinate and more than adamantine hardness of the French'. Henry roundly declared that he would not leave his voyage for any negotiations that his ambassadors might undertake. The winter of 1416-17 was spent in preparations. At least £136,000 was to be provided by taxes upon laity and clergy, more loans were raised and stores accumulated. Some of the orders have a pleasant sound. In February 1417 the sheriffs of England were ordered to have six of the wing feathers plucked from every goose (except breeders), packed and sent to London for the fletchers winging the arrows. By the end of July 1417 the force assembled numbered some 10,000 effective fighting men (possibly about 12,000 crossed in all), and, as before, 1,500 vessels were procured to convey them. Henry hired a good many from the obliging Netherlands; Genoese craft were also chartered and, to the indignation of the Great Council, a number of

Venetian traders were pressed into the English service. On 23 July, 1417 the force started to embark. Its destination was secret.

It was a more far-sighted and experienced commander who now led the second expedition. The tactics were not to be those of the Agincourt campaign. Henry had made up his mind to seize Lower Normandy before working his way up the Seine valley and appearing before Paris in such overwhelming strength as to bring the Armagnacs to terms. He had decided to winter in France; and as he was proposing to annex territory, he could not strip the countryside bare. Whilst the weather held, he must make all the progress he could, getting as many supplies as possible across the Channel for an army that could not be allowed to alienate the inhabitants by pillaging the farms and villages, and must therefore be substantially provisioned from home. Lower Normandy was clearly the right area for such operations, for, if the sea-routes were well protected (to the Earl of March was assigned the task of 'skimming the sea'), victuals and materials, to say nothing of drafts to replace casualties, could be brought over in large quantities from Southampton to the base which Henry intended to establish at Caen. That was his first objective, while the dauphin, who had his army at Rouen, could be watched, and any possible threat from him forestalled, by patrolling the main roads eastwards. Henry landed at Touques near

Harfleur on 1 August, 1417. The Duke of
Clarence was immediately sent up the river
Touques to reconnoitre at Pont l'Evêque and
Lisieux. After waiting a week for reports of the
dauphin's movements and finding everything
clear, Henry moved upon Caen. Turning southwards along the Dives and then westwards to
the south of Troarn, he picked up Clarence on
the Lisieux-Caen road and sent him forward to
seize the suburbs. Fortunately for posterity the
duke was able to occupy St. Stephen's Abbey,
the monastery of the Conqueror's foundation,
before the monks who had determined to fire it
carried out their project. Meanwhile, the Earl
of March, who had landed at La Hogue, joined
the king at Caen and the place was closely
invested.

The town fell to a continuous series of assaults
on 4 September, and the castle surrendered
five days later. Caen was thoroughly plundered
so as to strike terror into the surrounding district, most of which came into Henry's hands by
the end of September. In the meantime John
the Fearless carried out the first part of his plan
of co-operation by moving to the Oise, in order
to cut off Paris from upper Normandy and
Picardy. On 5 September he crossed the Oise
and assaulted Pontoise, which fell on the 11th. He
was counter-attacked and had to yield some of
the territory won, but by the middle of October
he had got Montlhéry as well as Chartres with

its neighbouring fortresses. His movements round Paris kept the Armagnacs wholly occupied and effectively prevented any move against Henry V.

But he had gone further than Henry expected. If John carried his strategy a little farther and made Paris his real target, and along with Paris secured the person of Charles VI, difficulties were bound to arise. Having smashed the Armagnacs, he would in the end find himself opposed to Henry, the claimant of the French throne. Nor did he underrate Henry as an opponent. For the time being therefore, political considerations determined the plans of both confederates. Now that the Duke of Burgundy was active around Paris, Henry could not sit down comfortably in winter quarters at Caen: his course was to absorb as much of Lower Normandy as he could without risking a lengthy siege at any strong place. The first move was south-east, via St. Pierre-sur-Dives and Trun, to Argentan which quickly capitulated, and the momentum took him on to Verneuil. The advance guard got as far as Alençon, and the fall of that place opened the way into Maine and alarmed Anjou. The Angevins could get no help from Armagnac quarters, and consequently made, along with Brittany and Maine, a separate truce with Henry (16 November, 1417). Potential dangers in the west and south-west were thus eliminated. As a buffer in the south-east between the English forces and the Burgundians stood the Armagnac fortresses of Dreux and Evreux; the position being reasonably stabilised in this quarter, Henry could begin the siege of the powerful fortress of Falaise. Although the town capitulated on 20 December, the castle itself did not give in till 1 February, 1418. Its capture [1] ended the first phase of operations in Normandy.

The task ahead was to hold what had been already won and to subdue the western areas of the duchy. A series of expeditions secured the greater part of Western Normandy. Gloucester was sent through Vire into the Cotentin: his objective was Cherbourg and his route lay through Torigny, St. Lô (occupied 12 March, 1418), Carentan and Valognes—names in the *bocage* country famous in the 1944 operations. Supplementary to this was the expedition of the Earl of Huntingdon against Coutances which capitulated on 16 March, 1418. There could now be a southward advance along the Cherbourg-Avranches road, while contact was established with Gloucester's force to the north by the occupation of Piron, La Haye du Puits and Barneville. Avranches appears to have been occupied by the middle of April. Another task force under the Earl of Warwick was sent southwards up the Orne to Domfront which it had been resolved to capture by blockade rather than

---

[1] 'The capture of Falaise marks a great historic step forward to final victory'—General Crerar, 17 August, 1944.

direct assault. It was in English hands by 22 July. Alongside of this southward activity, English forces began to press forward along the Caen-Paris road; for by the spring of 1418 Henry was so well established in Normandy that he could afford to take the war eastwards. On 8 June, 1418 Louviers was besieged; it had surrendered by the 20th and Henry could send an envoy to the Armagnac captains at Ivry and Dreux to negotiate their surrender.

The move towards the Seine in the early summer is explained by momentous events in Paris. On 29 May the Burgundians under L'Isle Adam entered the city by treachery and took prisoner, among others, the Count of Armagnac, who was shortly afterwards put to death. In addition to the capital, they secured possession of the Oise fortresses on the north, and the castles of the Upper Seine on the south. Henry need no longer mark time to see what John the Fearless was going to do. The duke had taken alarm at his progress in Normandy and saw himself threatened by the inexorable Englishman. It was now to be the policy of Henry's unreliable ally to rally his Armagnac opponents in opposition to the English on the Seine and to strengthen the more important remaining Norman garrisons against the invader. Two such crucial points were Rouen and Pont de l'Arche above it on the river. In 1944 Pont de l'Arche was one of the main crossings place of the Allied Expedi-

tionary Force in their north-eastward drive
(18 August), while Rouen, which could for the
moment be by-passed, was not entered till a
fortnight later. In 1418 Henry was not pursuing
an enemy force retreating to the Rhine, but was
faced with the need to establish a great base
astride the Seine alike for operations in northern
Normandy and for a move up the river to Paris.
To capture Pont de l'Arche and sever communications with Paris was the necessary preliminary
to an attack on Rouen. Pont de l'Arche could
not be taken by a frontal assault and it was found
necessary to cross to the north bank. The English
had brought up pontoons and light craft, and
by making a noisy diversion lower down the
stream they got a strong party over without the
loss of a man (14 July). The French irregulars
whom they found on the other side were commanded by the Lord of Chastellux, who had just
helped to seize Paris for John the Fearless, and
Henry at once sent to ask the duke for an
explanation. When it came, the position was
left in no possible doubt. The duke was preparing
to fight for Rouen, and the Armagnac admiral
Robert de Braquemont had been commissioned
to negotiate with the Burgundian captain of
Rouen with the object of forming a united front
against the English. Henry need not hesitate
any longer. 'Like all the French', growled the
chaplain in 1416, 'he (John the Fearless) will be
found double-dealing: one man in public, another

in secret'. The crude English forecast had proved right.

Rouen was now directly in danger; in Paris it was realised that its fall would probably mean the loss of the duchy. The city had already sent a force of lances and archers into the Norman capital, which made all preparations to resist until the Duke of Burgundy arrived to relieve it. Would he come? He had entered Paris on 14 July ; but once there, he could see that the situation was not as favourable as he had hoped. The Armagnacs controlled both the Marne and the Seine through the possession of Meaux and Melun, while they commanded the roads from the southwest at Montlhéry. They could thus interfere with the provisioning of the city and raid right up to the gates. On 21 July, 1418, they seized Compiègne where they placed a garrison strong enough to control the trading routes into Picardy. Both for the sake of Paris as well as to free Normandy from the English, the duke had to come to an agreement with his Armagnac opponents. His efforts resulted in the temporary agreement of St. Maur-des-Fossés (16 September, 1418) by which the duke and the dauphin were to make common cause against the enemy. In the end the dauphin could not be brought to ratify it; but the negotiations were enough to warn Henry of the dangers that he was likely to meet. He was careful not to go further up the Seine until he was absolutely sure of Lower Normandy and the great castles still holding out there were in his hands. These were Cherbourg, Domfront, Mont St. Michel. Domfront had fallen at the end of July, but Cherbourg held out against Gloucester's 3,000 troops for five months. Deep ditches cut in the underlying rock guarded it on the south side, where the American forces approached it in 1944, a powerful castle was on the north, and on the east the bridge spanning the entrances to the harbour had been destroyed. It had to be tackled from the sand dunes on the west, where the besieging forces were exposed to a hail of projectiles from the guns of the town. Mining and other siege tactics proved of little avail; blockade was the only possibility and the place did not ask for terms till 22 August, 1418, the surrender (if no help came) to take effect at Michaelmas. It was a most valuable fort for western Normandy, and not until its fall and the release of the besieging forces could Henry bring all his effectives to bear against the Norman capital.

To Titus Livius, the humanist in the service of Humphrey of Gloucester; to the anonymous biographer of Henry, identified, though wrongly, by Hearne as Thomas Elmham; and above all to the English soldier, the admirable versifier John Page, who was evidently in Gilbert de Umfraville's contingent, the English account of the siege of Rouen is due. It lasted from 30 July, 1418 to St. Wulfstan's day, 19 January,

1419, ending, not by any direct assault or breach of the walls, but by the starvation of the inhabitants. The besieging forces could not seal off the city from the outside until St. Catherine's Abbey to the east of the place had been wrested from the enemy. When the circle was completed, the order was roughly this: the king had his headquarters for civil business in the Charterhouse about a mile outside the walls on the eastern side; his fighting headquarters were near the Porte St. Hilaire on the N.E. of the town. The two northern gates, the Porte Bouvreuil hard by the castle and the Porte Beauvoisine (both giving their names to the northern *faubourgs* of the modern city) were watched by the earl marshal and the Duke of York; to the west of the town could be seen the standard of Clarence flying from the ruined abbey of St. Gervaix; the flat ground south of the river was guarded by the Earl of Huntingdon and Thomas Montagu, Earl of Salisbury. Of the latecomers, Warwick, who had successfully taken Caudebec so as to prevent supplies being sent up by river to the besieged, was posted at the Porte Martainville not far from St. Catherine's Abbey; and when Gloucester arrived from Cherbourg he was given command at the Porte St. Hilaire, nearer to the walls than the royal headquarters. The strangest sight to the French must have been the 1,500 Irish kernes under Thomas Butler, Prior of the Hospitallers at Kilmainham, near Dublin. They

wore no breeches, had one foot bare, and carried
for weapons a circular shield, darts and a knife
rather like the Gurkha kukri. Excellent foragers,
as troops they were an unmitigated nuisance.

A medieval siege on such a scale was a heraldic
event. The checking and verification of coats of
armour had been done by Clarence before the
expedition sailed, and the heralds knew the exact
location of every shield. Henry was extremely
particular about these matters, and would not
permit the assumption of arms. Only those who
had borne arms (i.e., armorial bearings) at
Agincourt were exempted from the rule. But
he had many more important things to think
about: the clearing of the river from all enemy
craft, the digging of trenches for the protection
of his troops, the fixing of stakes in front of his
positions, the establishment of communication
between each of the four main divisions, the
placing of his artillery. As at Harfleur and
Agincourt, he had every detail at his fingers'
ends. And he had to keep guard against any
possible relief. But for all the promises made to
the city, the Burgundians never came. The joint
forces of the duke and the dauphin that lay at
Pontoise were riddled with disaffection, short of
pay and food, and in the end found themselves
compelled to move to Beauvais for lack of victuals.
It was to Beauvais that the men of Rouen made
their last cry for help as starvation drew nigh
before Christmas.

At the approach of the English forces the population had swollen because of the large number of persons admitted into the city gates from the suburbs and neighbouring country. As the siege progressed the captain, Guy le Bouteiller, was forced to eject many of the *bouches inutiles* into the ditch surrounding the town, where they could die a lingering death of starvation. Even then there were too many inside, and it was hunger that ultimately (31 December, 1418) brought the captain to ask for terms. At each gate the French shouted to the English, but only at the southernmost did the cry fall on listening ears. It was Gilbert de Umfraville who took the message, 'and thei thanked God and our Lady that thei had mette with hym; for he was of the old bloode of that countri of Normandye'. The request was passed on by the other English captains to the king, who consented to receive a deputation from the town. Umfraville warned the Roueners to speak guardedly:

> Theynke with hert byforn youre tonge,
> Lest your tonges byn to longe.

What in fact they said nearly wrecked the negotiations, for Henry was in a grim mood and not to be moved by the plight of the 'poor pepull' in the ditch ('I put hem not there, and that wot ye'). He would hear no talk of a

136

surrender conditionally upon the King of France
and the Duke of Burgundy being informed and
failing to bring aid, for they knew all along of
the plight of Rouen and had refused help. But
after an explosion of anger at the garrison for
having

> kepte my cite
> the which that is myn heritage free

he consented to treat. Discussions went on in
an atmosphere of wrangling for a fortnight:

> We asked mykill [much] and thei proferid
> small,

and were finally broken off, to the fury of the
townspeople who threatened to burn the gates
and admit the English rather than continue the
siege for another day. Their determination to
surrender overbore their negotiators, and on
13 January, 1419 a settlement was reached,
partly through the intervention of Archbishop
Chichele, who came down from St. Catherine's
to mediate with the clergy of the city. If no help
arrived by 19 January, Rouen was to submit
wholly to the king's mercy, pay 300,000 crowns
and surrender all war material. The Normans
in the garrison were to be held as prisoners; but
any citizen prepared to take the oath of homage
to the king was to retain his property. The city

was to enjoy all the privileges it had before the reign of Philip VI.

The terms were reported to the King and Queen of France, and to Duke John the Fearless, who blamed the dauphin for not bringing up troops, and blandly advised the Roueners to make the best terms they could. After this extraordinary display of supineness, he moved on to Provins, where he stayed another four months. Most of his army had been disbanded. It is clear that the agreement of St. Maur was a dead letter, and that all action to save Rouen had been paralysed by the jealousy and rivalry between the dauphin and the duke, fostered by the pro-Burgundian queen. Finance may also have been a potent cause of strife, for both sides lacked money to pay their troops, and in such an atmosphere mutual recriminations flourished.

Henry made his entry into Rouen on 20 January, 1419. As at Harfleur and in the London procession after Agincourt, he refused to make the occasion a personal triumph: but John Page does not let it go unrecorded:—

> He rode upon a browne stede,
> Of blake [black] damask was his wede.
> A petrell of gold full bright
> About his necke hynge down right.
>
> To the mynster did he fare
> And of his hors he light there.

his chapell mette him at the dore,
and went before him alle in fere,
and songe a responde full glorious
'Quis est magnus dominus?'

The people of Rouen had none of the spirit of
the *résistance*. Most were quite content to accept
Henry as their duke and as their king. No more
than nine persons were exempted from the royal
pardon, of whom only the captain of the cross-
bowmen was executed. A substantial body of
Norman knights and squires submitted to Henry
after the capture of Rouen, and the bulk of the
clergy proved equally compliant. Many captains
of castles and local *seigneurs* did not wait to be
overrun, but surrendered quickly. On the roads
northwards from Rouen to Dieppe and Neuf-
châtel, places like Longueville, Torcy, Arques
and Nesle came over before the end of January,
as well as the fortresses between Dieppe and
Harfleur. On 5 February Mantes capitulated
to Clarence: on the 8th Dieppe opened its gates:
the conquest was radiating both north and south-
east.

It might be imagined that with all this solid
progress, Henry would not have troubled about
negotiating with his opponents. To find him,
therefore, entering into the most elaborate conversations during the siege of Rouen may give
the reader a shock. It led Dr. Wylie, for instance,
to suppose that at this point his position was less

favourable than it appeared on the surface; that even if Henry had merely held on to what he had already got in Normandy and had advanced no further, he would have found difficulty in paying his troops, whereas deeper penetration into hostile territory would have involved him in constant hazards. But Henry had adequate supplies of men and money both for garrisoning Normandy and for fighting further into the interior. The point has been well stated by Dr. Newhall:

> The chief advantage enjoyed by the English king lay in the fact that while his opponents were financially embarrassed most of the time, he had a sufficiency of money. This enabled him not only to raise an army, but to keep it under his control as well.

The remarkable thing is the volume of support which he received from England. Both parliament and convocation did their utmost in voting taxes for him: in 1417 his prestige stood at its highest, and when he was away abroad he was not felt to be an absentee king. In the lamentation for Henry V which John Harding, years after Henry's death, inserted in the first version of his chronicle, occur the words

When he in France daily was conversant,
  His shadows so oboumbred [sheltered] all
    England

That peace and law were kept continuant
In his absence full well through all the land.

It was not till the spring and summer of 1421
that the stream began to run dry, and the king
had to resort to extensive borrowing in which he
was largely helped out by his uncle, Bishop
Beaufort. Even in the period of reaction against
direct taxation, 1422-1429, the financial burden
of the war was mainly thrown upon Normandy
and upon 'the conquest'. It will not do, therefore,
to exaggerate Henry's financial problem in
1419, although, as the English government was
presently to find, there was a limit to the squeezing
of Normandy. The true explanation of Henry's
readiness to talk with the dauphin is otherwise.
Henry was a political soldier: he ran fighting
and diplomacy together. Of Maria Theresa, in
the first partition of Poland, Frederick the Great
once remarked '*Elle pleurait et prenait toujours*':
Henry negotiated and kept on taking. The taking
was to stimulate the enemy to improve his offers.

As soon as Rouen had fallen, Burgundian and
Armagnac, as if they had learned nothing from
the past four years, started to bid for Henry
more ardently than before. A personal meeting
between Henry and the dauphin was arranged
for 26 March, and in the meantime an armistice
was arranged to cover all the country between
the Seine and the Loire. But on the day the
dauphin could not be induced to appear: he

may have heard from the envoys who met the English representatives during the siege of Rouen, that Henry was still determined that the Treaty of Brétigny should be accepted before he could waive his claim to the French throne. But with Burgundy relations were more promising; it was at the negotiations with the duke that Henry first saw—and kissed—the Princess Catherine who came to Meulan on 30 May, 1419, in company with her mother, Queen Isabel, and the duke. Henry was enraptured. He had already received Catherine's portrait and had formed high hopes of her. But his desire for the princess could not conquer his hard-headed determination to maintain, whatever happened, his absolute right to Normandy and to the territory covered by the settlement of Brétigny. According to the chronicler of St. Denys, the Earl of Warwick told the French that if Normandy and Aquitaine went wholly to Henry, the king would consent to peace and to marry the princess. These conditions the French found excessive— and the English proceeded to take Gisors and Pontoise. The latter, so much favoured in the past by Burgundy and the queen, was won by a stratagem on 31 July, 1419. Henry called it the most notable capture he had made outside Normandy. It was one of the keys to Paris.

The loss of Pontoise was heavily felt in the capital, already suffering from scarcity of food. It added yet another hostile force to those already foraging in the district, and made the inhabitants only the more anxious that the dauphin and the duke should meet and make the earlier compact of St. Maur-des-Fossés a reality, pacify local enmities, and lay plans for driving back the English. The dauphin, when approached by the Parisians, wrote to the Duke of Burgundy suggesting that a meeting should take place on 26 August at Montereau, where the Yonne joins the Seine. The dauphin was present on the day named, but the duke raised difficulties which seem only to have been removed when the dauphin offered to hand over his castle there. The interview was held on 10 September in a fenced enclosure beyond the barrier at the end of the castle bridge. What words passed is unknown, but the duke fell and died under the blows of an axe, victim of an Armagnac plot, the leader of which may very well have been Tanneguy du Chastel.

The murder of Duke John the Fearless was one of those acts which precipitate rather than alter the course of historical events. More than a hundred years later the Carthusian prior of Dijon observed that through the hole in the duke's skull the English entered France. Henry saw the implications at once: it meant victory— and the Princess Catherine *que tant avoms desiré*. It meant that all opposition to him as the invader of France and claimant of the French throne would be swept away by the wave of moral indignation against the dauphin, who had completely put himself out of court: it meant alliance with Burgundy—a veritable alliance this time—and the support of Charles VI and Isabel in avenging the murder and establishing peace with France.

The young Duke Philip of Burgundy was supported in his desire for treating with Henry by important members of his family and by the towns of Artois and Flanders. But if he and they sought Henry's friendship, they must be told the truth. While expressing sorrow at the tragedy of Montereau, Henry told the duke's envoy that there must be no repetition of his father's double-dealing. If Duke Philip did not come into line by Martinmas 1419, he would go on with his conquests alone. After these strong words, he told them what was in his mind. He was agreeable that Charles VI should, during his life, retain his title as King of France and Queen Isabel her estate, provided that, upon Charles's death, the crown of France should fall to him and his heirs, and that in the meantime, since Charles was ill, he himself should govern the country. He would marry Catherine and no charge should fall upon the parents. If the duke was prepared to agree to these proposals, he would do his best to see that the murderers were punished, and also arrange for the marriage of one of his brothers to a sister of the duke. When the Burgundian envoys demurred to dealing

with such big questions, Henry made it clear
that he was not delivering an ultimatum, but
outlining the principles of a proposed agreement.
If, however, the Duke of Burgundy had designs
upon the French throne, he would make war
upon him to the end. Henry's plain speaking
is the measure of his exasperation with the
murdered duke. Henceforth he would tolerate
no tergiversation.

The project for alliance with England was
formally put to an assembly of prominent
Burgundian supporters at Arras on 17 October,
1419. It was energetically supported by the
people of Paris, who did their best to further the
Anglo-Burgundian coalition. At the council that
day Paris declared itself in favour not only of a
truce, but 'a treaty and alliance with the king of
England'. Doubtless the reason was expediency:
the 'most circumspect' men of Paris, as Henry
called them, were engaged in making the best
terms they could for their (now) Burgundian city
within the framework of the proposed alliance,
and they had no intention of raising pedantic
objections or making difficulties for Henry.
Monstrelet reports the issue of the debate on
that October day. In favour of the alliance was
the argument that Henry and Philip together
would be able to unite all Frenchmen in a firm
union; in opposition. it was urged that if they
took Henry as an ally, he might seize the opportunity to drive out the king, the queen and all

the French governing elements and establish
barons, knights and clerks from England in their
place. The 'saner part' rejected this bogey and
the alliance was agreed upon. It was embodied
in a formal treaty, sealed on 25 December.
This was the essential preliminary step to the
greater treaty between France and England which
followed.

Chapter Eight

The Treaty of Troyes

THE Treaty of Troyes, already outlined in the
negotiations with Burgundy, might have
been one of the most fateful documents in English diplomatic history—had Henry V survived
to complete his conquests. It was made in two
stages. The first was when on 9 April, 1420,
English envoys met the French king and queen
and the Burgundians at Troyes, and the principal
terms were settled. By them, England and
France were to enter into a new partnership.
Upon the death of the French king there was to
be one dynasty, the house of Lancaster, adminis-
tering, through the respective national organisa-
tions, the two countries. Charles and Isabel
were to retain the state and dignity of king and
queen of France during the former's lifetime;
upon his death, the French crown was to belong
to Henry and his heirs for ever. The dauphin
was cut clean out of the succession, and Henry
was to be styled 'heir of France', besides being
regent owing to Charles's infirmity. This union
was to be consummated in the marriage of Henry
and the Princess Catherine, who was to receive,
Henry promised, the dowry of an English queen,

40,000 crowns a year. The English king undertook to reduce to obedience all parts of France still subject to the dauphin. While Charles lived, these conquests were to be to the profit of the French crown (of course controlled by Henry); after his death, Normandy (now held in full sovereignty by Henry) along with the 'conquest' was to be subject to it. In the territory so conquered those persons obedient to Charles VI who were willing to swear to the treaty should be restored to their possessions unless Henry had already granted them away. A further clause stipulated that fit and proper officers were to be appointed to govern the kingdom, which was to be ruled according to existing laws and customs: the authority of the *Parlement* was to be maintained, and all corporate bodies such as churches, colleges and universities were to be maintained in their privileges. The great barons, the estates and notable communities of France were to swear that they would leave 'our said son Henry power and exercise of ruling the commonwealth'.

At the second stage (21 May) when the councils of Henry and Charles VI and Duke Philip deliberated jointly, these provisions were confirmed and issued, along with others, by Charles VI in a solemn and final document. There were two riders and an entirely new clause. Provision was made for Catherine in the event of her widowhood; it was agreed that compensation from conquered dauphinist lands should be made to Burgundians whose property had already been confiscated and given away by Henry; and (the new clause) that Henry should try to secure from the three estates of both England and France the declaration that when he should become King of France, the crowns should be united in the same person, while each kingdom retained its own laws and neither was subject to the other. The two countries were to have perpetual peace, a defensive alliance, and freedom of trade, saving the customs. A chance was also given to the allies of either side to avail themselves of any benefits of the treaty that might affect them, within eight months. Finally, none of the contracting parties was to enter into any negotiations with the dauphin save by the consent of all and also of the estates of both kingdoms.

Three points in the treaty deserve special notice. First, the vagueness of the territorial clauses. By one of these Henry V was given a free hand to seize what he could of the lands still subject to the dauphin. He was therefore committed to an indefinite war of sieges and operations against fortified islands of territory in enemy hands. The main strength of the dauphin lay south of the Loire and in Languedoc: but he still had a good many powerful outposts around Paris, e.g. Dreux, Montereau, Meaux, Melun, while in north-eastern France his supporters were strong in Champagne, were in occupation of Compiègne and Guise, and in a position to hinder communications between the Burgundian territories and Paris. Even if in the north-east Burgundian sympathies were fairly general, the dauphin had also his friends, and several Burgundian captains, notably Louis Bournel and Jacques d'Harcourt, Count of Tancarville, had deserted a long allegiance. Harcourt was particularly awkward, since he seized St. Valery-sur-Somme and other places in that river valley and conducted an active war on the English by land and sea.

In the treaty no definite approval is given to Henry's claim to hold Normandy in full sovereignty. Not a word is said about this, and later on Duke Philip of Burgundy was to deny that it had been admitted at all. So completely may Henry have regarded Normandy as his own duchy (in spite of the clause assigning it, on Charles VI's death, to the French crown) that his occupation may have been treated as *de jure*, not *de facto*, and hence the omission to make its status clear. In any case, however, the line between Normandy and 'the conquest' seems to have been very vaguely drawn. Some of the places later conquered, like Dreux, were placed under the administration of Norman *baillis:* the jurisdiction of the English *bailli* of Mantes extended to places within twelve miles of Paris.

In the second place, the crucial position of

Burgundy. Not only the acquisition of dauphinist territory, but the maintenance of the treaty itself depended upon the good will and co-operation of the Burgundians in France. This was no easier in 1420 than it is among the United Nations of the present age: perhaps even more difficult. In the Middle Ages the English were not good collaborators with Frenchmen. In the field misunderstandings tended to occur. Just before the treaty there was an awkward incident (January 1420). After Roye had surrendered to a Burgundian force and the lives of its garrison had been spared, the dauphinist defenders were returning under safe conduct to Compiègne: an English force under the Earl of Huntingdon and Sir John Cornwall fell upon them, slaughtered many and took others prisoners, although the English had been instructed to help in the recapture of Roye and might have been expected to co-operate with the Burgundians. John of Luxemburg, their commander, naturally protested, and in an angry scene John Cornwall struck one of the Burgundian captains.

Huntingdon distinguished himself on another occasion, when with the Burgundian forces he was besieging Sens, by refusing to treat with the town's ambassador 'who had a great beard' which was 'not the manner of the English'. Treating could not proceed until the offending thicket had been shaved off. Later, after the surrender of the town, delayed for such ridiculous punctilio, the English created great offence by declaring that they were 'les plus fors' of the two allies. More serious was the attitude of those who had originally been carried into support of the English alliance by indignation against Duke John's murder, but later felt the revulsion spreading among the upper classes against any such pact with the foreigner. At the siege of Melun the Prince of Orange withdrew for such a reason. According to Jean Juvénal des Ursins, when Henry asked him to take the oath to the Treaty of Troyes, he is alleged to have replied that

> 'he was ready to serve the Duke of Burgundy, but that he should take an oath to put the realm into the hands of the ancient enemy, that he would never do'.

The chronicler Monstrelet, himself a member of a noble family, is obviously divided between his Burgundian sympathies and his dislike of the English régime.

Yet it will not do to exaggerate. Duke Philip retained many of his lords as active participants in the war against the dauphinists. Monstrelet notes the presence of many of the French nobility with Henry at the siege of Meaux; the captains of Flanders, Artois and Burgundy flocked to help the duke and the English forces at the relief of Cosne-sur-Loire just before Henry's death. A Burgundian figure like Gilbert de Lannoy was one of the king's most faithful supporters. Councillor and chamberlain to the Duke of Burgundy, he worked and fought for Henry V both as soldier and as diplomat. The regent sent him through northern Europe and the near east as his agent in 1421, and Gilbert, on his return, symbolised his double alliance by sending an account of his travels both to the King of England and the Duke of Burgundy. His brother Hugh was used by Henry in negotiations for a treaty with the King of Castile, and in 1422 Bedford made him captain of Compiègne. But it was the personality of the king which held people loyal to the alliance. All his contemporaries were impressed by his power of discipline. He punished all transgressors of his orders instantly and without mercy, and so, in the words of Monstrelet 'was so dreaded and feared by his princes and knights, captains and all kinds of people, that there was no one, however near and dear to him, that dared break his ordinances, especially his English subjects: and those of the kingdom of France who were under his obedience, whatever their rank, were equally reduced to this'. In Paris, apart from the highest officers, most of the administrative posts were given to Burgundians, chiefly loyal and long-standing members of Charles VI's household: the government of the city remained essentially French in composition.

Thirdly, the union of the two kingdoms. This

was not a rigid administrative unity, but a dynastic superiority binding the two peoples, each governing itself under its own laws and customs. As a symbol of this, ratification by the two parliamentary assemblies was to be sought. Obviously in the absence of clearer definition it would scarcely be possible to compare with the Troyes settlement the proposed Act of Union propounded by the British to the French Government on 16 June, 1940, one clause of which ran:

> The two governments declare that France and Great Britain shall no longer be two nations but one Franco-British Union. The constitution of the Union will provide for joint organs of defence, foreign, financial and economic policies. Every citizen of France will enjoy immediately citizenship of Great Britain, every British subject will become a citizen of France.

Yet it may be noted that the union suggested after the Germans had occupied Paris and the British Expeditionary Force had been evacuated from Dunkirk, was a closer one than any foreshadowed by the Treaty of Troyes. Interchange of citizenship is, needless to say, a modern concept and may be left aside: but joint organs of defence or of policy (there was no suggestion of an amalgamated Council) were not contemplated, and in this respect the Anglo-French kingdom of the Treaty is no less remote from the old Angevin Empire of Henry II with its genuinely Anglo-French personnel and its community of diplomatic practice.

The English control was exercised only at the highest level. In Normandy the seneschal, treasurer, king's military lieutenant and admiral, were Englishmen. So also were the *baillis* and the captains and lieutenants of the garrison: but the civil officers of lower rank, the *vicomtes* and *prévôts* were uniformly French. There were Frenchmen in the treasury at Caen, and in the *chambre des comptes* or exchequer. No attempt was made to introduce English institutions into the conquered lands. Apart from Harfleur and Cherbourg, Normandy was not to be made an English colony. When the estates of Normandy were summoned to Rouen, Henry treated them with consideration. He did not attempt to lay taxes on his French subjects without their assent, though he maintained the ordinary indirect taxation of the French kings, notably the *gabelle*. In the same spirit he abstained from foisting an English clergy upon the church in Normandy. Professor Waugh has observed that among the very numerous appointments to ecclesiastical offices or benefices recorded in the Norman rolls for 1421 and 1422, there are only twenty in favour of men with what seem to be English names, and only three of these concern parish churches. Among the higher clergy at the time of the conquest Henry's supporters were the bishops of Coutances, Avranches, Séez and Bayeux, within Normandy; and those of Beauvais, Chartres, Thérouanne, Troyes and the archbishop of Bordeaux, without: but frequently recurring vacancies complicated the position, and Henry was not anxious to have Frenchmen in the Norman sees. The two archbishops of northern France, Louis d'Harcourt of Rouen and Regnault de Chartres of Rheims were hostile; and Gerard de Montaigu, Bishop of Paris, was a leading upholder of the dauphin, whom he bravely called 'le seul fils et seul héritier du roy'. Montaigu died in September 1420, but Henry's attempts to secure the see for a member of the Burgundian Council was wrecked by the opposition of the chapter of Notre Dame, who in December elected Jean Courtecuisse, a leading conciliar and opponent of Anglo-Burgundian co-operation. Courtecuisse had to leave Paris for a year and live at St. Germain-des-Près for safety because 'he was not pleasing to the King of England'. It was not until June 1422 that Henry arranged with Pope Martin V for Courtecuisse to be translated to Geneva, when a Burgundian partisan, Jean de Rochetaillée, took his place. On the whole, the Paris chapter was an exception; and far less difficulty was experienced with the abbeys and priories. Professor Newhall estimates that although the temporalities of about two thirds of the abbeys and monasteries were at some time under English administration, ultimately sixty-six at least out of the ninety-seven supposed to exist in Normandy during the early fifteenth century took the oath of fealty and had their temporalities restored.

No contemporary chronicler accuses Henry V of favouring the English. His stern treatment of offending compatriots was a source of admiration and wonder. But the new order was a severe one for any that sought relations with the dauphin or with any parts of the country under his obedience. Between occupied and unoccupied France a great gulf was fixed. To receive private and wholly unpolitical correspondence from territories below the Loire was enough to condemn a man to banishment, and any harbouring of strangers and friends from unoccupied France might lead to serious penalties.

Whatever may have been the case in the early years of the settlement, in the end the treaty proved an expensive business for England. The theory was that the territories acquired should pay for the war. But after Henry's death, when the Duke of Bedford had become regent, increasing penetration of English forces into dauphinist areas threw a heavy burden upon the duchy of Normandy, since the newly conquered lands were too devastated to contribute much. A more cautious policy would have been to ensure inner tranquillity throughout Normandy and to hold the frontiers strongly without going further afield. But, as has been pointed out, the treaty envisaged a long series of attacks on hostile points, and, for this purpose, increased levies on Normandy, as well as the employment in France of troops which could better have been utilized on the Norman frontiers. The levies produced discontent in the duchy; and the drawing off of its garrisoning troops elsewhere opened it to attacks from the south. In time the Norman contribution proved inadequate and had to be met by subsidies from the English exchequer: which for England meant more loans for the immediate payment of troops and more taxation. Even in Henry V's last year of campaigning (1421-2) the contribution of Normandy and the 'conquest' to the cost of operations came to no more than £70,000 (Tours), or between £10,000 and £11,000; and Henry spent a good deal more than that. Financially therefore, whatever may be said on other grounds, the union of the two countries was a liability for England.

A contemporary popular song depicts the Princess Catherine, after bemoaning her fate and repelling her English husband, as crying

> Retourne-toi, embrasse-moi
> Mon cher Anglais!
> Puisque Dieu nous a assemblés,
> Faut nous aimer.

The French, who had accepted Henry, had to make the best of it. But the dauphinist comments take us back to 1359. 'All the country on the other side of the river Loire (wrote Jean Juvénal des Ursins of occupied France) is black and obscure, for they have put themselves into the obedience of the English. But that country (beyond) remained pure and clear in the obedience of Monseigneur le Dauphin'. Alain Chartier considers the settlement as 'outrageous and disloyal folly'; Jean Chartier holds that the English have occupied the realm 'without reason' and that the oath of allegiance to the King of England is 'degrading and criminal'. The south of France opposed the treaty from the first; but the discouragement of the defeat was great, and seven years were to elapse before the flame of France burned once more, kindled by a peasant girl from Domrémy in Champagne.

Chapter Nine

The Last Two Years

ON the day when the Treaty of Troyes was sealed, Henry was betrothed to the Princess Catherine: on Trinity Sunday (2 June) he was married to her in the cathedral of Troyes by the Archbishop of Sens. There was a great banquet next day, but Henry declined any further festivities: he would start at once, with Catherine, on his campaign for the reduction of the dauphin-ist fortresses. First Sens, then Montereau; then down the Seine to Melun. Here, unlike the other places, he found the town united with the garrison in the determination to resist, and for four months the place kept him at bay. There were Scots inside, and Henry brought James I of Scotland with him to call upon his compatriots to surrender—but in vain. It was a difficult place to take, for it lay on both banks of the river with the castle on an island in midstream. The siege was remarkable for the exploits of the miners on both sides: fights went on in the subterranean galleries that were dug out, and only starvation led the defenders to capitulate (18 November, 1420). Henry had twenty of the Scots hanged for disobedience to their sovereign.

After the fall of Melun Henry made an imposing entry into Paris (1 December), to be followed next day by Queen Isabel and Catherine. During the siege of Melun Henry's queen had first stayed in Corbeil, but later Henry had a house built and furnished for her near his tent, where she remained for a month. Every day at sunrise and sunset English minstrels sang and played for her entertainment. The visit to Paris was not, however, a purely social one: Henry wished to be present when the States General ratified the Treaty of Troyes. In the 1359 negotiations they had declared that they would prefer 'to endure and continue to endure the great confusion in which they lived rather than that the kingdom should be thus weakened and defrauded', and proceeded to reject the conditions which King John had accepted. In 1420 the estates 'believing and reporting the said peace to be praiseworthy, necessary and useful to both kingdoms and their subjects and also to the whole of Christendom ... approve, praise, accept and authorise the Peace ... fully and faithfully for themselves and their successors'. Henry requested and received a declaration that all refusing to swear to the treaty should be treated as rebels; and there were also proceedings to be taken against the men charged, in their absence, with the murder of John the Fearless, notably Arnaud Guillaume, lord of Barbazan, and Tanneguy du Chastel.

From Paris Henry went on to Normandy for a visit of nearly three weeks, in order to extract a grant from the estates and to hear their grievances. He was on his way back to England which he had not seen for nearly three and a half years: but too late for the parliament which met on 2 December, 1420. It was rather a quiet assembly, for no money grant was demanded, since, as the Chancellor explained, the object was to advise the king and provide remedies especially touching the poverty of his subjects and the scarcity of money in the land. The council evidently felt that for the time being taxation had gone as far as it could: but certain petitions put forward by the commons redeemed the record from dullness. They were concerned with the recent treaty and the king's new status. The commons asked that no parliament summoned by the king's lieutenant (when Henry was overseas) should be dissolved because of the king's return, as it seemed likely that 'for the good government of France just as much as of England he may be sometimes here and sometimes abroad as shall seem best to his wise discretion'. Secondly they successfully petitioned that the statute of 14 Edward III c.3 be reenacted, declaring that the crown of England should never be subject to the crown of France. Evidently in view of Henry's title 'heir of France' they thought that the precaution was necessary. Thirdly they requested that petitions presented

by them in the present parliament to the lieutenant (the Duke of Gloucester) should not,
before being engrossed, be sent overseas for the
royal assent, but should be disposed of as far
as possible within the realm during parliament,
and that any left over should be treated as void:
this ordinance to hold good in all parliaments
henceforward. No answer was given to the first
of these petitions, and the third was politely
declined. Both were framed so as to expedite
business and to prevent petitions being delayed
by the royal absences abroad. Their failure
is typical of Henry's determination to keep
as much English business as possible in his
own hands while he was in France. Nothing
better illustrates the character of his government.

Passing through Amiens and Calais, Henry
and Catherine landed at Dover on 1 February,
1421. The welcome was tumultuous. Livius
recounts that the barons of the Cinque Ports
waded into the water and bore the king and
queen on their shoulders to land (travellers were
often carried in thus—it is the bearers who are
important). The first halt was very properly
Canterbury, where Chichele received them.
Henry then went on ahead to London, but the
official welcome did not take place till the
queen arrived on 21 February, when the city
put on its heraldic splendour as at the return
from Agincourt and similar choirs of apostles,

martyrs, confessors and virgins sang Catherine into the capital of her new realm. On 23 February she was crowned in the Abbey, enthroned in the palace of Westminster, and feasted (without her husband, for it was her day) in Westminster Hall, where the menu consisted entirely of fish courses and confectionery. The fish, one authority has remarked, included 'almost every denizen of fresh or salt water that is ever seen on a modern table'. These junketings over, Henry started upon a tour of the principal towns of his kingdom which took him and Catherine (who had joined him by 15 March) through Bristol and Shrewsbury to the Midlands, and then by way of Nottingham and Pontefract to York, whence he paid flying visits to the shrines of Bridlington and Beverley.

It was a pilgrimage, Walsingham says, to holy places. Most of the municipalities visited happen to have figured prominently in the returns made to the Lollard commissioners in 1414, and Henry may have wanted to ascertain the feeling of the townsfolk, in addition, we are told, to hearing the complaints of the poor and doing justice to the oppressed. But there was a more cogent reason: he wanted money, and a personal visit to the counties would help him to extract it, particularly if pressure was brought to bear. Unwilling that people should connect the treaty with an immediate demand for a subsidy, he had decided not to ask for a grant in the next parliament, but to get what he could by loans. A promise had been given to Charles VI that he would return with reinforcements by midsummer, 1421; by 13 May he had collected £38,000 in advances (Beaufort contributed the enormous sum of £17,666), and in addition the convocation of Canterbury voted him a tenth. When parliament met (2 May) the Treaty of Troyes was duly ratified; and so high stood the prestige of the king that it was decreed that any statute or ordinance which might be made while he was away on his next expedition to France should only hold good until the next parliament after his return. Henry was anxious to keep the governing authority of the kingdom in his hands: he had no objection to interim measures taken while he was abroad, but he claimed to exercise the right of censorship and revision when he was back. His lieutenant in the realm was obviously on a short tether.

His authoritarian temper, and his determination to have complete control over church and state alike are illustrated by two episodes that occurred during this brief spell at home. The first concerns his relations with his uncle, Henry Beaufort. The Bishop of Winchester stood in wealth and influence far above the ordinary diocesan. An invaluable member of the Council, periodically chancellor, he had given Henry great assistance both as prince and as king. But a man who could lecture Clarence or Gloucester was not easy to control: he had the mounting ambition of a Wolsey, joined with high financial and administrative abilities. Like his early predecessor Henry of Blois (also of royal stock), he had done his best to make his see independent of Canterbury: but he wanted more than this. In the autumn of 1417 Beaufort found himself at the Council of Constance. It was given out that he was on pilgrimage to Jerusalem, and he came in pilgrim's guise; but it was his intervention and the formula he propounded that solved the problem which the Council had been debating: whether to agree on a scheme of reform before proceeding to the election of a new Pope, or to put the election first. Beaufort proposed immediate election and the reference to the new Pope, as his primary task in the Council, of the main points of reform on which the nations were agreed.

The new Pope, Martin V, evidently in recognition of what he owed to Beaufort, a month after his election conferred a cardinalate upon him and empowered him to act as permanent legate *a latere* in England. Archbishop Chichele at once protested to the king against an innovation which threatened to overshadow the authority of the Archbishop of Canterbury as papal legate in England, and Henry, much incensed, had the papal bull containing Beaufort's legatine commission impounded. Undeterred by the royal indignation, the tough and arrogant prelate held on, and obtained a fresh bull. He had thereby infringed, in the most serious way possible, the Statute of Provisors (1390), and the king, who had his uncle's movements watched by Thomas Chaucer, made it perfectly clear to him that under this the penalties would be the forfeiture of his goods and degradation from his see. Beaufort got as far as discussing with Chaucer (who was in the bishop's confidence as well as in Henry's) the possibilities of disappearing from the country altogether—once more on a pilgrimage to the Holy Land—as well as the question of his successor at Winchester; but Henry who had made his determination to resist Beaufort's cardinalate and legatine commission perfectly clear, was prepared to give his uncle time and not to force him to extreme courses; and in the end Beaufort had to accept the facts and smooth his own future by making Henry the enormous loan noted above. While he lived Henry would have no emissary of the Holy See permanently in England for fear of papal demands for taxation as well as from a determination to maintain the Statute of Provisors which Martin was doing his best to overthrow. All these negotiations Henry kept entirely secret: they survive only in private letters and the memoranda of the agents appointed to watch the bishop's behaviour, which Mr. McFarlane has recently brought to light.

The second of these episodes touches the reform of the English Benedictines. While Henry was on his tour of the country between February and April, 1421, he received complaints about the laxity in the monasteries of the order. Determined that a remedy should be found, Henry wrote, under his own signet of the eagle (16 March) to the abbot of Bury St. Edmunds as the most important prelate of the order, bidding him summon a General Chapter of the English Black Monks. The abbot respectfully referred him to the two presidents of the order as the competent authority, and at his request the Chapter was convened for 7 May: at which, according to Walsingham, there were present 60 prelates and over 300 monks, doctors and proctors. At the beginning the king was present and addressed the Chapter 'on the early religious observance of the monks, on the devotion of his ancestors and of others in founding and endowing the monasteries, and upon the negligence and carelessness of the moderns'. He besought them to reform, and assured them how much confidence he placed in their prayers.

This was no rhetoric, for the king relied especially on the suffrages of the religious, particularly at critical moments like the battle of Agincourt. ('Now is all England praying for us', he is reported to have said in the early morning of 25 October.) Henry had prepared thirteen charges against the order, which were put forward by his representatives and discussed in committee. All, in their original form, were rejected by the monks, but in place of them the abbot of St. Albans brought forward seven which he and his colleagues agreed to observe. It is characteristic of Henry to initiate the reform himself rather than through highly placed seculars whose intervention would have been suspected by abbots of the status of Thomas Spofford of York and John Whethamstede of St. Albans. His charges show that he had studied the Rule of St. Benedict, as well as the statute of Benedict XII against property-holding. The drafting may have been done by the Carthusian prior of Mountgrace, but the method of approach and the underlying spirit of the criticisms are the king's. No English monarch since Edgar had been prepared to undertake such a task, but Henry's determined piety was not to be stopped by lack of precedent.

On his way back from visiting the shrine of St. John of Beverley Henry received news that must have given him a shock, though he betrayed no sign of emotion: his brother Clarence had been killed by the dauphinists at Baugé. The enemy had recently been reinforced by a considerable number of Scots, who with the dauphinist forces had cut off Clarence on the southern frontier of Normandy. They took advantage of a raid carried out by the duke in force through Maine and across the Loir to muster on his line of retreat to Normandy at La Lande Chasles, a village about six miles south-east of Baugé.

Clarence was unaware of their presence till his scouts on 22 March brought in some captured Scots. Taking far too small a force with him, Clarence, against the advice of his best captains, set off in pursuit, and was drawn on into a hand-to-hand fight with greatly superior numbers, over 5,000 to his 1,500. In the mêlée Clarence, the Count of Tancarville, Lord Roos and the faithful and attractive Gilbert de Umfraville were slain, and the Earls of Huntingdon and Somerset taken prisoner. Fortunately Clarence had left the Earl of Salisbury behind; too astute a soldier to be caught on his backward march in the same place as Clarence, Salisbury made a detour to cross the Loir at La Flèche, and escaped over the Sarthe at Le Mans. The lamentations of Henry's biographers for Clarence cannot conceal the fact that he did a very foolish thing, unworthy of a man of his fighting experience; if the French had been able to catch Salisbury as well, the English position in Normandy would have been seriously endangered. But they lost their chance, and permitted Salisbury to reorganise and even, in retaliation, to raid Maine and Anjou.

Baugé had, however, a considerable moral effect. A dauphinist revival was threatened and Henry made speed to return to France. He crossed to Calais in order to put Picardy 'in better governance' by capturing places still in enemy hands. But having got there he heard that the dauphinists had advanced through Perche upon Chartres and were besieging the place. Quickly he changed his plans and hastened to Paris. The situation had been growing more critical, now that the dauphin's forces had taken the field again, and there was little time to lose. Henry did not stay long in Paris, but joined the main English force which at the end of June was along the Seine between Mantes and Meulan. He was about to lead it to the relief of Chartres, when he heard (8 July) that the dauphin had relinquished the siege and retreated into Touraine. The excuse the latter gave to the people of Lyons was lack of supplies and unhealthy weather, which, given the strength of the Chartres garrison, made a successful outcome of the siege unlikely. He did not consider that Henry, who had only brought over 4,000 men, was really formidable. Henry followed him towards the Loire. The first objective was Dreux, in enemy hands a stronghold that constantly threatened Normandy, and one which, if captured, would help to secure communications between Normandy and Paris. After a three weeks' siege, Henry took it (8 August, 1421), with the result that minor fortresses between it and Chartres quickly surrendered. But the dauphinist forces refused to be drawn into a battle. After taking Beaugency (but not its castle), the king marched slowly up the right bank of the Loire to the suburb of Orléans, but was not strong enough to attack the city itself. It was a hot month and his troops suffered badly from dysentery. On 18 September he reached Nemours, and on the 22nd Villeneuve-le-Roy on the Yonne, which was recovered after a brief siege. If the results of the expedition in terms of territory won are not striking, Henry had at least recovered the prestige the English had lost after Baugé.

Unable to make the French face him in the field, Henry turned to the reduction of dauphinist fortresses in northern France. He had determined to employ the winter in the reduction of Meaux, since Melun fell the most formidable enemy centre in the neighbourhood of Paris. Built on a loop of the Marne, Meaux was a place of exceptional strength. The river cut the city into two parts, the town on the northern side, and the market, protected on three sides by the river and already practically a fortified island, since a canal cut through the peninsula. The besiegers were hampered by a heavy flood, and later by sallies from enemy cavalry. For five months the town held out: when it fell, the market had still to be assaulted and the ferocious defenders held on till 2 May, 1422, extending Henry's skill and ingenuity to the uttermost. He had been preparing to float down the Marne a large wooden tower placed upon two barges lashed together, a tower matching the height of the walls to which it could be grappled by a drawbridge. The tests, made when the market had given in, proved highly successful. Meaux was treated with some severity, though no more than justice was done to its ruffianly defender the Bastard of Vaurus. All English and Scots fighting in the garrison were to be at the king's mercy, as well as any who had participated in the murder of Montereau.

The chronicler known to historians as the Pseudo-Elmham observes that of all Henry's sieges this was 'the most harmful.' Large numbers of English died of dysentery in the cold weather and the king himself contracted the illness that was later to carry him to the grave. It was the last big operation he undertook. There seems little evidence for the statement that he had been ailing long before the siege; for with one exception his campaigning had not been of the sort to undermine his constitution. That exception was the march to Agincourt; but a great part of his time in the second French expedition was spent in diplomacy and administration. He was certainly stricken now. When Meaux fell he moved to Paris to meet Catherine, now the mother of his infant son. The royal pair spent Whitsuntide in great pomp at the Louvre, but after a fortnight Henry felt obliged to seek country air at Senlis. It was here, at the end of July, that the Duke of Burgundy appealed to him to counter-attack the dauphinist forces besieging the Burgundian garrison at Cosne-sur-Loire. Hard pressed, the garrison agreed to surrender on 10 August, if no help was sent. For motives of policy Henry was particularly anxious to give all possible assistance to his ally, and started off in a litter, too weak to ride. At Corbeil he was so weak from the dysentery that he had to hand over command to the Duke of Bedford. One more effort he made, at Charenton, to take his place at the head of his troops, but he could not sit his horse for long, and was carried to the castle of Bois de Vincennes outside Paris.

He knew that he was dying, and in his masterful way made all preparations. His last days he spent in conversation with the men he trusted most: his brother John, the Duke of Bedford; his uncle, Thomas Beaufort, Duke of Exeter; Richard Beauchamp, Earl of Warwick; Sir Lewis Robsart, and a few others. Some of his actual words, as they were remembered, are given by his biographer:

It is certain that according to the will of our Saviour, to whom be praise, honour and thanks, I cannot avoid death which, according to the condition of all human flesh, is upon me. If, therefore, during my reign I have ruled otherwise than I ought, or done any injustice to anyone (which I do not believe), I ask his pardon. For the good services done me, particularly in this campaign, I thank you and your other fellow-soldiers; for which, if death had not cut short my intent, I proposed to reward each of you with fit recompense according to his deserts. I exhort you to continue in these wars until peace is gained; and I protest before God that I was not drawn into them by any ambitious desire for domination or vain-glory or worldly honour, or any other cause save only that by prosecuting my just title I might obtain both peace and my own rights; and I had been, before they began, most fully instructed by men of holy life, perfect and prudent, that I could and should enter upon them and bring them to a conclusion with this object in view, without danger to my soul.

To my brother, the Duke of Bedford, I here decide that the custody and government of the duchy of Normandy shall be committed till my son reaches years of discretion. Let my brother, the Duke of Gloucester, be protector and defender of England. I desire that my uncle, the Duke of Exeter, my chamberlain, and Sir Walter Hungerford the steward of my household, shall be attendant upon the person of my son, whom may God in His mercy bedew with his supernal benediction.

The king then gave them a long and astute discourse 'on the just and right ways they were to follow and the method of government they were to observe'. He showed them his will with the later codicils in which he had directed how his father's debts were to be paid and had provided for the reward of members of his own *entourage*. Thereafter he paid no further attention to business, but made ready to receive the sacrament and extreme unction. As he was passing, the little group of magnates and clerks caught the words 'Thou liest, thou liest! My portion is with the Lord Jesus', as if he were boldly addressing the evil spirit, and at the end, as his lips touched the crucifix: *In manus tuas Domine ipsum terminum redimisti.* 'And within that said castle on the last day of August, the tenth year of his reign, in commending his spirit with gentle gesture into the Saviour's hands, you could have thought that he had fallen asleep rather than breathed his last'.

The last instructions are very typical: the concern for his commanders; the exhortation to fight on till full peace—which the treaty had not brought; the assurance about the purity of his motives and his reference to the support given by churchmen to his dispute with France, recalling the lines (*Henry V*, Act 1, Sc. ii):—

> K. Hen. May I with right and conscience make this claim?
>
> [Abp. of] Canterbury. The sin upon my head, dread sovereign!

Whatever was actually said at Bois de Vincennes, the different versions given in more of less contemporary accounts point clearly to the dangers which Henry foresaw when he made his dispositions and followed them with a long lecture on English politics. Monstrelet's version is that Bedford was to hold the regency of France unless the Duke of Burgundy was willing to take it. This is probably quite correct, for to Henry's mind Burgundy must be treated with the utmost consideration; significantly too, Monstrelet makes the king advise his followers to avoid dissension with Burgundy at all costs. But the main difficulty concerns Gloucester's position in England. The English Brut chronicle and the *Life* state that Henry had nominated Gloucester as protector and defender: both accounts were written after Duke Humphrey's title had been decided by the Council in England: but in his third will (10 June, 1421) Henry had devised the regency of England, were he to die prematurely, upon Gloucester. He may have changed his mind and, as one contemporary account suggests, given him some sort of joint guardianship along with Bedford, Exeter, and Bishop Beaufort. At all events, when Henry was dead, the Council declined to let him have either regency or custody, and only accorded him the limited military title of Protector and Defender; while the effective government was left within its own hands. Against this decision, which must have been very largely due to Beaufort, the Duke of Gloucester was to struggle in vain; and the greater part of Henry VI's minority was to be disquieted by the rivalry and tension between uncle and nephew, both of whom compromised themselves in various ways and were each conscious of the other's weaknesses.

The English reaction to Henry's death was one of universal lamentation. There were extraordinary scenes at every stage of the six weeks' mournful and magnificent journey when the king's body, with the giant effigy in boiled leather on top of the coffin, was borne to its final resting-place in the Abbey. More significant is the reaction of the French and of French writers both within the 'conquest' and in the unconquered territories. All, whether normally hostile to Henry or not, pay impressive tribute to his love of justice. One of the fiercest critics, Chastellain, wrote that Henry was above all 'the prince of justice, both in regard to himself for the sake of example, and in regard to others according to equity and right; he gave support to none out of favour, nor did he suffer wrong to go unpunished out of regard for kinship'. Both dauphinist and Burgundian agree that the fear he inspired in all coming into contact with him made him instantly and universally obeyed and assured of good service; and Jean Juvénal later (1454) summed him up in a realistic way by saying that 'no prince was more fitted to conquer, acquire and guard what he had conquered than he'. To Jean Chartier Henry is the *subtil conquérant*— perhaps the best description of Henry's mixture of diplomacy, fighting and administration.

The French have always been prone to self-analysis. In the fifteenth century they gave two explanations of Henry's victories. The first contends that the English successes were not the outcome of superior military skill so much as the inevitable result of the divisions within the kingdom. This is the line taken by the pro-Burgundian Bourgeois de Paris, who declared that the King of England would never have dared to set foot in France had it not been for the dissensions caused by the unhappy name of Armagnac: 'and Normandy would still be French, nor would the noble blood of France have been shed nor the lords of that kingdom exiled'. But among the many who deplore the divisions as the cause of the invasion, one, Alain Chartier, sounds another note:

> We have given our enemies victory over us by lack of decision and lack of courage rather than that their prowess has acquired it for them.

In other words, it was the spirit of consistent and continuous resistance that was lacking. This diagnosis can be found in the remarkable tract, the *Quadrilogue invectif*, and in a significant class of literature, the complaints of the people against the nobility. In these, bitter protest is made against the nobles who care nothing for the economic destruction of the realm and make no serious attempt to evict the English. To the nobles in 1414-1422 they attribute what modern French patriots have attributed to their financier-politicians of 1939-40. In popular eyes, the nobles were more concerned about their own comfort than about fighting the enemy. Even thirty years later, when the English garrisons had departed, Jean Juvénal des Ursins, Bishop of Beauvais and aged adviser to Charles VII, could say the same thing in his *Remonstrances au roy pour le reformation du royaume*, when he dealt with the personnel of the army. Both the prince and his captains must be *vaillants*; and he drew a distinction between *vaillance de courage* which implies discretion—a mixture of courage and determination used at the right season—and *hardiesse*, the quality that brought Clarence to his end. *Vaillance de courage* is not confined to the so-called 'military' classes, and Juvénal advocates the use of artisans, craftsmen and technicians in the army of his day:

I, being Bishop of Beauvais, when I have been on a strongly defended frontier, have seen and known charming companions, experienced in feats of arms, who were both valiant and bold, spring from the stock of labourers and artisans, men who bore themselves as valiantly as the others; and sometimes, in various situations in war, they are even more useful, for they know better how to endure pain and live under primitive conditions.

Juvénal has much to say about the knights: the gist of his remarks is that they must be men of

energy and hard work, not *oisiveté*. No gentleman
is of such high birth that, if he is slack, a good
varlet should not be preferred to him; and when
war is over, knights should not disdain to make
their own harness, shoe their own horses, build
their own houses and do their own carpentering.
Instead of being maintained in idleness or roam-
ing about as a menace to the countryside, they
should be settled as farmers on the land and
engage in manual work just like the agricultural
labourer or the artisan.

The fact that these criticisms were written
about 1454 gives even more point to them in
relation to the last years of Charles VI. At the
same time no amount of *vaillance de courage* nor
democratization of the army could immediately
avail against the adverse political situation in
which France found herself at Henry V's death.
A great part of the English strength was derived
from successful tactics of encirclement. Though
Sigismund had proved a broken reed when called
upon, England gained greatly from the alliance
of 17 April, 1423, with John V of Brittany and
John I, Count of Foix, who acted as a counter-
poise to the dauphinists in the south. In May,
1423, Bedford married Anne of Burgundy,
Philip's sister, and the Duke of Brittany's brother,
Arthur de Richemont, also married into the
house of Burgundy. In the south an alliance
between Foix and Comminges kept the dauphinists of Toulouse on the alert. In Champagne an

offensive by the forces of Salisbury and John of Luxemburg seemed likely to threaten the Rhone valley. On 17 August, 1424, Bedford with the banner of the dual monarchy won at Verneuil a decisive and crushing success over the dauphin's troops, at last brought to a pitched battle. This was probably one of the most desperate moments in the history of France.

Yet in ten years time Bedford was dead and Philip of Burgundy preparing to be reconciled to the 'roi de Bourges' now crowned as Charles VII. That Henry's work should perish in thirteen years when the political and military situation was so predominantly favourable to him at his death indicates one of the outstanding revivals in French history. There are some who will point to the Maid of Orleans and declare that she performed the miracle. This is not the whole truth : but she did one supreme thing. She gave Charles confidence in his legitimacy, made him understand that he was the true and undisputed King of France; and in and by her death at English hands she broke through the web of intrigue, the manœuvring for position, which disgraced his *entourage*, and showed what the inspired tenacity of the French countryman could do.

The history of France is full of magnificent pages on which the triumphs of her genius are written in fire for the wonderment and profit of all. But the shining periods, as well as the years

THE LAST TWO YEARS

of labour that produced them, are interspersed
with stretches of dissension and disillusionment.
The intensity of her effort seems to impair for
a time a nervous system capable of supreme
response and superb energy. Yet this is the
rhythm of a people intent on high moments,
strivers after glory, to whom politics are a constant
essay in transformation.

Chapter Ten

Epilogue

PEOPLE accustomed to constitutional democracy find it hard to transport themselves into an age when a king went to war for his rights, and his claim needed only the backing of the more influential of his subjects: an age when as yet it is scarcely appropriate to talk of 'the government'; for government, in the broader sense, develops from the king's household and may continue there, even when the greater departments have gone 'out of court'. It is only very slowly that representative elements are brought into the system. A further difficulty meets those who have studied a certain amount of early English history: they will have frequently seen it stated that the House of Lancaster ruled by parliamentary title and were upholders of constitutional principle. To such, Henry V is likely to prove a trifle disconcerting.

Of late years there have been many assaults upon this 'parliamentary' view of the Lancastrians. It is gradually becoming recognised that Henry IV was a shrewd, patient and entirely determined ruler who was by no means the constitutional paragon that he has been thought.

Much more is this true of his eldest son, brought up in the dynamic atmosphere of border warfare, with small opportunity for relaxation and the arts of peace. In his small council of warrior magnates Henry V takes us back to the Dukes of Normandy, most of all to the Conqueror himself, with his firm grasp on Church and State. Nor were contemporary ideas of the royal power as advanced as some of our growing institutions seemed to imply. In the middle of the fifteenth century Sir John Fortescue, Chief Justice of the King's Bench, can argue in support of the Lancastrians that the kingdom is real property, capable of descending to the heir of the preceding king. True, the king is more than a private person— he holds a public office. Yet he is proprietor of his kingdom. So to another distinguished lawyer in 1441 it appeared that the law courts, even the court of parliament, were the king's inheritance; and it was argued that taxes in parliament were the revenues of his court and thus equally a hereditament.

What then were the duties of a king? His honour and his office were not held for nothing. In a recent study of the king's estate, a leading constitutional historian has cited a contemporary verse which seeks to explain the meaning of the gold and jewelled crown the king wears:

What doth a kynges crowne signifye,
Whan stones and floures on sercle is bent?

185

Lordis, commouns, and clergye
To ben all at on one assent.
To kepe that crowne, take good tent [heed].
In wode, in feld, in dale and downe,
The leste [least] lyge-man, with body and rent,
He is a parcel of the crowne.

In other words the crown is the guarantee of
unity and cohesion in the body politic. Its
holder's duty is summarized by Fortescue: 'Lo!
to fight and to judge are the office of a king'.
Bellare et judicare. The great thirteenth-century
jurist Bracton put the popular view in the same
way: 'in the king who rules rightly these two
things are needful, namely arms and laws, by
which he is able to govern both occasions, war
and peace'. The power of justice the king holds
in order to keep the peace and maintain his
subjects in their rights. And as he has no earthly
superior to defend his own right, when attacked
he must, if justice be denied him, resort to arms;
for the king's war is a legal trial by battle,
wherein he seeks the right which he cannot
obtain by peaceful means. But he must essay all
peaceful expedients first.

The letter which Henry V wrote to Charles VI
from Southampton on 28 July, 1415, when the
transports were getting ready, carried this legality
to its highest pitch: it so captivated the monastic
chronicler of St. Denys that, he says, 'I thought
it worth inserting to embellish my history'

186

(*ad venustatem historie*). In it Henry makes one more appeal to Charles. 'We are not so blinded by fear that we should not be ready to fight for the justice of our cause: but the law of Deuteronomy [xx. 10] has ordained that whoever prepares to attack a city must first offer it peace'. This the king now does. 'We exhort you in the bowels of Jesus Christ, according to the perfect teaching of the gospel *Friend, pay me what thou owest*, and in order that the deluge of human blood be saved, that restitution be made of the inheritance and of the rights that have been cruelly taken away from us or at least of those which on previous occasions through our ambassadors and envoys we have already demanded of you and with which we are content out of respect for God and in the interests of peace'. Finally, Henry professes himself ready to reduce the figure demanded for Catherine's dowry by £50,000, if this would lead to a settlement, preferring 'to have the rights which generations of our predecessors had left us, along with Catherine, rather than to multiply treasure with the maximum of iniquity and suffer the crown of England to be disinherited'.

The last touch is interesting: he would rather moderate his demands and have his historic rights than be wealthy and be denied his inheritance. Absolute confidence in the justice of his claim to the home of the Norman kings; complete trust in his admirably prepared case against the cruel detainer of his lands who refused to do him justice: these convictions on the part of the king communicated themselves to his whole *entourage*, especially the hard-bitten young brothers, true sons of Henry IV. Their loyalty and their belief in him can have been awakened by no sudden conversion such as popular tradition describes, but must have developed as they perceived his serious and passionate purpose, and have been stimulated by his irresistible grace and energy. After the queer Richard and the bleak Henry Bolingbroke, romantic appeal returned to the crown. The clergy felt it and gave Henry V a testimonial which the Confessor might have envied. Henry's daily devotions, the governance of his chapel, his liturgical interests, his sympathy with the best elements in the religious orders, his confidence in the prayers of his people captivated the Church. Here was the Just King, with a united kingdom behind him, conscious of the righteousness of his cause, who was confronting an enemy state distracted by partisan interests, lacking the solidarity of a true kingdom, and governed by men that were constantly converting (to borrow the phrase of Commines) *le bien publique* into *le bien particulier*. To write him down as predatory and unscrupulous is to judge him without his diplomatic inheritance and without reference to his opponents. Powerful, magnetic and subtle he certainly was: if he pursued one end, he could see how all sorts of remote contingencies might affect it, and he would vary his methods accordingly. Of propaganda he was a master; he knew how to use his own person to create an impression, to convince or to terrify. Ruthless he certainly could be: but there was no streak of cruelty or sadism in his nature. His justice was of an Old Testament quality, but it was justice all the same.

It was the misfortune of France that she had little to oppose to this unified and aggressive island kingdom. Her court was more civilized, her tradition of learning superior, her intellectual figures incomparably greater. Whom, for instance, had England to put up against Gerson or d'Ailly? But she was living on memories of the Capetian past; she had a divided council; her taxes were collected with difficulty, and the princes of the blood were not punctual and disciplined servants of the crown, like Thomas Beaufort or John, Duke of Bedford, but independent appanage-holders, and the greatest of them, John the Fearless, was making love to the French queen and attempting to seize the effective power. If France's potential was vast, her political coherence was deplorably low; it was impossible to focus all the resources of the kingdom upon the task of evicting the English, once they were in. And why were they allowed in? Alone in the French Council Bernard of Armagnac seems to have realised that it was necessary to fight the English for control of the narrow seas; for, in the long

run, Calais, Harfleur and Cherbourg meant more
to this country than garrisons held along the
north bank of the Loire. French historians have
not been slow to see in this English control of the
Channel the beginnings of British imperialism
based upon sea-power. During the last thirty
years of the fourteenth century the French
government had made serious efforts to develop
its marine defences, and the Genoese were valuable
allies. Yet the fact remains that Henry should
never have landed in 1415, or, having landed,
should never have got back. Much of Henry's
diplomacy was directed to breaking down the
Genoese alliance and to preventing further
assistance to France from Castile—for it was
a Castilian fleet that transported the Scots to
France in 1419, and constituted a perpetual
menace to the English possessions in Aquitaine.

It has been argued that after the Treaty of
Troyes Henry could not have anticipated years
of fighting the dauphin, and that if opposition
had continued he must later have agreed to an
arrangement by which he waived his title to the
French crown in return for retaining his northern
conquests and the old English possessions in
Aquitaine. This view seems to neglect his dying
instructions to Bedford and his complete feeling
of superiority over the enemy. It is beside the
point to maintain that the settlement at Troyes
meant the prolongation of the medieval feudal
world into the Renaissance age of national states,

an affront to the sentiment of nationality that
was steadily growing in the middle ranks of
French society, as well as an intolerable burden
both for English finances and for English administrative personnel. To put back the clock to the
twelfth century would not have deterred Henry
in the least; for his deepest desire, stronger even
than that of holding 'his own' duchy of Normandy
in full sovereignty, was to unite the princes of
Europe in a crusade for the recovery of the Holy
Places, the project with which his father is
correctly credited by Shakespeare in *Henry IV,
Part* 1. In *Henry V* (Act v, Sc. ii) the expedition
is a little more distant:

> Shall not thou and I (Catherine), between
> Saint Denis and Saint George, compound a boy,
> half French, half English, that shall go to
> Constantinople and take the Turk by the
> beard ?

But the real Henry, on his death-bed, stopped
the chaplains as they chanted *Be favourable, O
Lord, to Sion: build thou the walls of Jerusalem,* with
the words: 'O Lord, though knowest that mine
intent hath been and yet is, if I might live, to
build again the walls of Jerusalem'.

Creative projects perish because the technique
people employ to carry them into effect is wholly
inconsistent with their purpose. History, like
men's minds, is full of contradictions. The
fruitful, vital idea of an Anglo-French polity
is associated with a conquest which scarred the

whole of northern France. To Henry's credit it must be said that the idea was not chimerical. Despite the misery caused by armies, the long struggle of England and France lacked the 'total' character of modern warfare, and, apart from certain critical battles, had become at times more a school of arms, a sort of knightly education, than a national conflict. Again, the English nobility mainly spoke, and certainly wrote, in French; and neither side had forgotten the Norman and Angevin past. The two courts had scarcely extricated themselves from the tradition of that high-born Anglo-French civilization in which men like Bertrand de Born and Richard Cœur de Lion moved with ease and a king like Henry III found such æsthetic enjoyment. The two king-doms had much in common, and they were not being asked to sacrifice their own peculiar institutions. But a settlement, however imposed, has to be carried out by both sides; Henry's prestige and greatness could not, after his death, prevail sufficiently to keep his Burgundian ally loyal, and in Charles VII, after the Maid had revealed and restored him to France as the true and consecrated king, Frenchmen of all parties recognised the symbol of their nation's unity. And underneath, in the substantial middle and lower levels of society, both countries were developing their own characteristic and exclusive ways of life and thought. The age of the *bourgeois* is the age of the national state.

SELECT BIBLIOGRAPHY

For general background, see J. Calmette and
E. Déprez, *La France et L'Angleterre en conflit*, Vol.
vii, Pt. 1 of *Histoire du Moyen Age*, in *Histoire
Générale*. Ed. G. Glotz. Paris, 1937; Jacques
D'Avout, *La Querelle des Armagnacs et des Bour-
guignons*. Paris, 1943; J. A. Wylie, *The Reign of
Henry the Fifth*, 3 vols. (vol. iii completed by
W. T. Waugh). Cambridge, 1914-29.

a. *Contemporary biographies:*

    Henrici Quinti Angliae regis gesta [The Chaplain's
    biography, to 1416]. Ed. B. Williams. Eng.
    Hist. Soc., London, 1850.

    Vita et Gesta Henrici Quinti. The Pseudo-Elmham.
    Ed. T. Hearne. Oxford, 1727.

    Titi Livii Foro-Juliensis Vita Henrici Quinti. Ed.
    T. Hearne. Oxford, 1716.

    The First English Life of King Henry the Fifth
    [written 1513 by the author generally known
    as the *Translator of Livius*]. Ed. C. L.
    Kingsford. Oxford, 1911.

b. *Contemporary Chronicles:*

    Brut, The, or *the Chronicles of England.* Ed. F. W.
    Brie. Part 2. Early Eng. Text Soc., Orig.
    Ser., 136. London, 1908.

    Chronicle of John Strecche for the reign of Henry V
    (1414-1422). F. Taylor. *Bulletin of the John
    Rylands Library*, Manchester, xvi. 1932.

    Journal d'un bourgeois de Paris, 1405-49. Ed. A.
    Tuetey. Paris, 1881.

Le Fèvre, J. *Chronique* (1408-35). Ed. F. Morand. 2 vols. Paris, 1876, 1881.

Memorials of Henry V [includes Elmham's *Liber Metricus*]. Ed. C. A. Cole. Rolls Ser. London, 1858.

Monstrelet, Enguerrand de. *Chronique* (1400-1444). Ed. L. Douet d'Arcq. 6 vols. Paris, 1857-62. Eng. trans. by T. Johnes. London, 1810.

Religieux de Saint-Denys. *Chronique* (1380-1422). Ed. L. Bellaguet. Vols. 5, 6. Paris, 1839-52.

Walsingham, T. *Historia Anglicana* (1272-1422). Ed. H. T. Riley. Rolls Ser. Vol. 2. London, 1864.

Walsingham, T. *The St. Albans Chronicle,* 1406-1420. Ed. V. H. Galbraith. Oxford, 1937.

Waurin, J. de. *Recueil des croniques et anchiennes istories de la Grant Bretaigne.* Ed. W. Hardy and E. L. C. P. Hardy. 5 vols. Rolls Ser. London, 1864-91.

c. *Modern biographies of Henry V:*

Kingsford, C. L. *Henry V, The typical medieval hero* (Heroes of the Nations Series). London and New York, 1901. 2nd edn. London, 1923.

Mowat, R. B. *Henry V.* London, 1919.

d. *Other modern works:*

S. B. Chrimes. *English Constitutional Ideas in the XV Century.* Cambridge, 1936.

The Register of Henry Chichele, Archbishop of Canterbury, 1414-1443, ed. E. F. Jacob. Vol. 1, Introduction. Oxford, 1943.

K. B. McFarlane. 'England: the Lancastrian Kings, 1399-1461', Ch. xi of *Cambridge Medieval History*, viii. Cambridge, 1936.

R. A. Newhall. *The English Conquest of Normandy*, 1416-1424. Yale and London, 1924.

Sir Charles Oman. *A History of the Art of War in the Middle Ages*, Vol. ii, 1278-1485. 2nd ed. London, 1924.

Charles Petit-Dutaillis. *The Feudal Monarchy in France and England*. London, 1936.

E. M. W. Tillyard. *Shakespeare's History Plays*. London, 1945.

T. F. Tout. France and England. *Their relations in the Middle Ages and now*. Manchester, 1922.

Index

INDEX

Hanley Castle, 56
Harcourt, Louis d', archbishop of Rouen, 156
Harding, John, 140
Harfleur (Seine-Inf.), 39, 67, 82, 93, 98, 101-2, 113-14, 116-17, 121, 135, 138-9, 155, 190
Harfleur (Seine-Inf.), siege of, 86-9
Harfleur (Seine-Inf.), surrender of, 90-1
Harlech Castle, 26
Hearne, Thomas, 133
Henry II, king of England, 7, 8, 22, 67, 155
Henry III, king of England, 12, 14, 69, 192
Henry IV, king of England, 3, 19, 21, 25-6, 30, 33-4, 63, 75, 184, 188
Henry V, king of England, Shakespeare's view of, 3-4; policy when prince of Wales, 21-2; birth of, 24; governor of North Wales, 24-7; story of his intention to usurp throne, 32-3; early 'wildness,' 36; appearance and personality, 36-43; dynastic discontent against, 44-5; Lollard rebellion against, 50-51; his punishment of the rebels, 51-2; Southampton plot against, 56-7; negotiating with France, 60-1; with Burgundy, 62-3; prepares for war with France, 74-8; loans raised by, 83-4; sails for France, 85; attacks Harfleur, 86-90; forces its surrender, 90-1; marches to Calais, 93-9; forced to battle at Agincourt, 99-100, 103-6; his disciplinary methods, 101-3; offers thanks for victory at Agincourt, 107-8; negoti-

ates with the Emperor Sigismund, 115-18; makes Treaty of Canterbury, 119-20; agreement with duke of Burgundy at Calais, 122-3; invades France for second time, 125 et seq.; how affected by Burgundy's movements, 128-9; besieges Rouen, 132-7; enters Rouen, 138; negotiates with the Dauphin, 141-2; relations with Philip, duke of Burgundy, after murder of duke John, 143-5; benefits under Treaty of Troyes, 147-50; loyalty of Burgundians to, 152-3; how Normandy was administered by, 155-7; marries Catherine of France, 160; besieges Melun, 161; enters Paris, 161; visits Normandy, 162; lands at Dover, 163; tours England, 164; raises money for new campaign, 164; attitude of, towards Henry Beaufort, 166-7; initiates reform of Benedictines, 167-8; returns to France, 170; besieges Dreux, 171; Meaux, 172-3; meets Catherine in Paris, 173; moves to Senlis, 173; last illness, 174; his last directions and death, 175-6; his body conveyed to Westminster, 178. Contemporary appreciations of, 178; estimate of his work, 184-9; his attitude towards France, 190; towards the Crusade, 191; his plan for an Anglo-French state discussed, 192.
Henry of Blois, bishop of Winchester, 166
Hereford, bishop of, see Polton, Thomas

201

INDEX

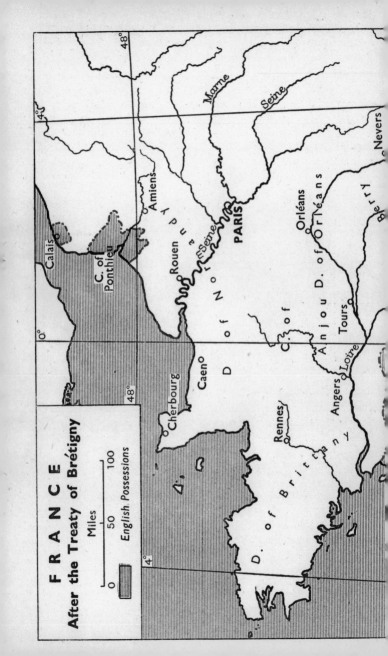

FRANCE
After the Treaty of Brétigny

Miles

0   50   100

English Possessions

Calais

C. of
Ponthieu

Amiens

Rouen

D. of Normandy

Cherbourg

Caen

PARIS

Seine

Marne

Seine

Nevers

Orléans

D. of Orléans

C. of
Anjou

Tours

Angers

Berry

Rennes

D. of Brittany

Loire